FEEL-GOOD FAMILY FOOD
DEAN EDWARDS

Also by Dean Edwards
Mincespiration!

FEEL-GOOD FAMILY FOOD

HEALTHY MEALTIMES MADE EASY

DEAN EDWARDS

BANTAM PRESS

LONDON · TORONTO · SYDNEY · AUCKLAND · JOHANNESBURG

Dedication

At the time of writing this book I lost three very special people in my life, people who were also very proud of me. This book is dedicated to my Gramps David 'The Bone' Phillips, Scott 'Shreds' Morrison and my Uncle Lionel. You are massively missed by everyone. xxx

TRANSWORLD PUBLISHERS
61–63 Uxbridge Road, London W5 5SA
www.transworldbooks.co.uk

Transworld is part of the Penguin Random House group of companies whose addresses can be found at global.penguinrandomhouse.com

Penguin
Random House
UK

First published in Great Britain in 2015 by Bantam Press
an imprint of Transworld Publishers

A CIP catalogue record for this book
is available from the British Library.

ISBN 9780593070871

Photography: Martin Poole
Design & art direction: Smith & Gilmour
Editorial: Jinny Johnson
Food styling: Aya Nishimura
Props styling: Tamzin Ferdinando
Proof reading: Elise See Tai
Index: Elizabeth Wiggans

Printed and bound in China

Penguin Random House is committed to a sustainable future for our business, our readers and our planet. This book is made from Forest Stewardship Council® certified paper.

1 3 5 7 9 10 8 6 4 2

CONTENTS

Family food

Eating, and food in general, has always played a huge part in my life. I've bordered on the obsessive at times, and I apologize to all the people I've bored to tears over the years, as I chatted about what I was planning for dinner. Some say I could send a glass eyeball to sleep when sharing stories about food!

The nostalgia that comes from sharing food in a family environment gives me a warm feeling, and I still cherish memories from my childhood when I was lucky enough to have amazing, healthy food, lovingly prepared by my parents and grandparents. If I'm honest, I took this for granted as a child, and when faced with a plate of greens or my mum's special mung beans my mind often wandered to potato shapes and turkey drumsticks. Much later I realized how fortunate we were to be fed so well and I promised myself that I would pass this on to my children if I was ever lucky enough to have them. Fast-forward to the present day and I am the adoring father to Indie-Roux, my beautiful little girl. Healthy family food is now top of my agenda and I've come up with a collection of family-inspired recipes which even the novice home cook can make with ease.

Whether or not my mindset on food changed because I became a father or because of the increasing bad press on convenient ready meals, I don't know. Perhaps I realized I had one last try at holding on to my youth! Whatever the reason, I can put a precise date on my eureka moment: 13th February 2012. This was when I decided that I needed to take a good look at the food I was putting into my body and cooking for my family. On that day I saw that all those years of eating whatever I wanted, whenever I wanted, had finally caught up with me. I was bang out of shape, in my mid-thirties and had to decide whether to continue down that route or do something about it. I didn't want to be the only dad in the park not able to chase my little one around, so I decided to clean up my diet and to start exercising again.

Like so many people, my health and well-being had become secondary to work and in any downtime I had I would indulge in my favourite pastime of lazing about on the sofa watching TV and eating junk. Sound familiar? I am so thankful for the choices I made and I now feel so much healthier. I have much more energy and am in the best shape of my life – and so are my family. I truly believe I've not only changed my own life but also my family's. And that includes the lives of future generations, as I'm hoping Indie takes this message on board. It's never too early to introduce your family to healthy home cooking.

I'm not a nutritionist, but I know what I should be putting into my body. My quandary was this: food has always been and will always be my great love, and so many of my pleasures have revolved around cooking and eating food – and still do. When I decided that I wanted to start eating more healthily I wasn't willing to compromise on flavour. I didn't want to be deprived of the joy of planning delicious meals to eat and enjoy with family and friends. I felt that a simple well-balanced diet, full of fresh ingredients, was the way forward. I used to think that foods laden with sugar and fats were the tastiest. In some respects that's true, but you can't tell me that a Thai salad with a zingy dressing isn't just as satisfying and good to eat as a fatty pie.

In fact I've found myself eating much more food than ever. Breakfast has become my most important meal of the day. Previously I'd either skipped breakfast or tucked into biscuits, chocolate and fizzy drinks. Horrendous, I know, but those extra ten minutes in bed seemed more attractive than getting up and making a quick and nutritious bowl of porridge or a smoothie. Now we all have a breakfast packed with goodness before we race out of the door in the morning, so why don't you try this too? For later in the day, try making your own healthier versions of your favourite takeaways. And have an amazing one-pot supper that takes minutes to cook and saves on the washing up.

I wanted my recipes to be fuss-free; meals that families could easily get on the table in as short a time as possible. With the meals in this book you and your family will eat well and you won't miss those high-sugar, fatty foods All this doesn't mean you can't cheat here and there – everything in moderation, right? But with this approach – a balanced diet packed with vegetables, lean meat, fish and fresh fruit, as well as other simple ingredients that are in your cupboard already or available from your supermarket – we can all make changes that affect our bodies both inside and out, and start feeling great! I know I do.

USEFUL TIPS

- Onions, garlic, shallots, potatoes and other root vegetables should generally be peeled before using, unless otherwise specified.

- I use medium eggs in my recipes, unless otherwise specified, and I prefer to cook with free-range eggs if possible, but that's up to you. I have suggested free-range in recipes where eggs are a main ingredient.

- Chillies vary in heat and not everyone loves them as much as I do! Feel free to use more or less chilli according to your taste. In some recipes I've suggested deseeding the chillies but again that's up to you.

- I love olive oil for some dishes and for salad dressings, but for cooking I'm using coconut oil more and more. Some diet experts are now saying that some refined oils aren't good for us, particularly when they're heated. Coconut oil is not expensive, it's easy to use and store and, just in case you were wondering, it doesn't taste of coconut. I've suggested using coconut oil in many of the recipes in this book so give it a try and see what you think.

CHAPTER 1
BREAKFAST

First off, let me tell you a secret. I NEVER used to eat breakfast. It wasn't unheard of for no food to pass my lips before lunchtime, as long as I had plenty of tea and coffee to see me through. An extra ten minutes in bed was preferable to starting the day right. If, on the odd occasion, I did eat something, I might pack away half a pack of chocolate digestives – and that's not an exaggeration. I will NEVER go back to those days. I wouldn't dream of sending my daughter Indie to school on a breakfast of biscuits so it's down to me to set a good example. Yes, we all tend just to grab a bowl of cereal or a slice of toast on occasion, but please be mindful of the amount of hidden sugars in most packaged cereals, and that's not even starting on all the frosted types.

You're probably sick of hearing that breakfast is the most important meal of the day, but here we go, breakfast really, really is the most important meal! We often to get our portion sizes wrong: small breakfast, if any, larger lunch, then have our biggest meal of the day at night. Try turning that on its head. What we eat in the morning sets us up for the rest of the day and gives us the energy to attack whatever life throws at us. If you skip breakfast you're going to be running on empty. No way are a couple of biscuits and a cup of tea, however nice, going to carry you through, and this leads to snacking.

Breakfast doesn't have to be hard work. A quick superfood smoothie or a big bowl of porridge takes no more than five to ten minutes to make and gives you a great start. And on lazier days at the weekend, nothing beats sitting down with the family and enjoying a cooked breakfast, such as my big breakfast frittata or very berry French toast.

If we're in a massive rush in the morning, as often happens when trying to get our daughter Indie to school before work, we love to grab some of this delicious granola with yoghurt and berries. Use this as a basic recipe, then add your favourite nuts, seeds and fruits. Look out for offers on nuts and dried fruits in your local supermarket. **MAKES 16-20 PORTIONS**

Fruity Cinnamon Nut Granola

2 tbsp coconut oil,
   plus extra for greasing
200g rolled oats
150g unsweetened
   coconut flakes
100g mixed seeds and
   berries, such as pumpkin
   seeds, sunflower seeds,
   dried cranberries and
   goji berries
50g almonds, crushed
50g pistachio nuts,
   shelled and crushed
2 tbsp chia seeds (optional)
40g dried apricots,
   finely chopped
100g raisins
1 tsp ground cinnamon
40g honey

1 Grease a baking tray and preheat the oven to 180°C/160°C Fan/Gas 4.

2 Put the coconut oil in a small saucepan and warm it over a gentle heat until melted. Meanwhile, mix all the dry ingredients in a bowl. Add the melted coconut oil and the honey and stir until everything is well combined.

3 Spread the mixture over the baking tray and bake in the preheated oven for 10–15 minutes. Remove the baking tray from the oven and leave the granola to cool. Crumble it into an airtight container to store.

4 Serve with fresh berries, Greek yoghurt and another drizzle of honey if you like.

These bars are ideal for a quick breakfast on the move while on the school run or on your way to work and they're also great enjoyed in the comfort of your own home with a cup of coffee. Be sure to cut the cooked mixture into bars before it cools or it will break up. If you do have any crumbly bits they're good sprinkled over fruit and Greek yoghurt! MAKES 12 BARS

Fruit and Nut Breakfast Bars

50g coconut oil, plus extra for greasing
150g rolled oats
50g mixed nuts and seeds, such as pine nuts, pumpkin seeds, sunflower seeds
50g dried fruit, such as cranberries and blueberries
40g dried apricots, finely chopped
2 tbsp unsweetened peanut butter
50g honey

1 Grease a 20cm, square baking tray with a little coconut oil, then line it with baking parchment. Preheat the oven to 180°C/160°C Fan/Gas 4.

2 Mix the oats, nuts, seeds, berries and apricots in a bowl.

3 Put the coconut oil, peanut butter and honey in a small saucepan over a gentle heat and stir until everything has melted together. Add this to the oat mixture, stirring as you go, then tip it all into the prepared baking tray. Spread the mixture evenly over the tray.

4 Cook the mixture in the preheated oven for 15–20 minutes. Remove the hardened mixture from the tin, then cut it into bars. Leave the bars to cool for a couple of hours before transferring them to an airtight container.

Porridge is definitely a favourite breakfast choice in our house, especially in the colder months. It really sets us all up for the busy day ahead, whether we're at home, work or school, as it's packed full of slow-release energy. Any berries work well, so try raspberries, strawberries or even some goji berries. **SERVES 4**

Super-start Porridge

160g porridge oats
500ml unsweetened
    almond milk or
    skimmed milk
500ml water
1/4 tsp ground cinnamon
2 ripe bananas, sliced,
    to serve
handful of blueberries,
    to serve
2 tsp runny honey or
    maple syrup, to serve

1 Put the porridge oats in a saucepan with the milk, water and cinnamon. Place the pan over a medium heat, bring the porridge to a simmer, then turn down the heat and continue to simmer for 4–5 minutes, stirring occasionally.

2 Serve the porridge in bowls and top with sliced banana, berries and a drizzle of honey or syrup.

DEAN'S TIP
For a change and to make your porridge extra nutritious, stir in 70g of crushed nuts, such as almonds, pistachios or hazelnuts, and 70g of dried fruit, such as raisins, cranberries or cherries.

This is a real breakfast treat for my family – my daughter Indie in particular loves this dish. It's also a good way of using up stale bread. I've suggested my favourite berries, but use whatever you like – frozen berries make a great standby when fresh ones aren't available. If you want a little extra sweetness, then drizzle over a little extra maple syrup or honey before demolishing your toast. **SERVES 4**

Very Berry French Toast

100g blueberries
100g blackberries
2 tbsp maple syrup,
   plus extra to serve
100g strawberries,
   hulled and halved
6 eggs
100ml milk
1 tsp ground cinnamon
4 slices of stale wholemeal
   bread (each about
   2.5cm thick)
1 heaped tbsp coconut oil
   or unsalted butter
4 tbsp low-fat Greek
   yoghurt, to serve

1 Place the blueberries and blackberries in a saucepan with a tablespoon of syrup and cook over a medium heat for 3–4 minutes. You want the liquid to be nice and syrupy so raise the heat if necessary for a minute or so. Remove the pan from the heat, stir in the strawberries, then set the mixture aside while you make the toast.

2 Beat the eggs in a bowl and add the milk, cinnamon and the remaining tablespoon of maple syrup. Mix well, then pour the mixture into a shallow baking dish. Add the slices of bread and leave them to soak for a couple of minutes, then turn them over and soak for a few more minutes.

3 Warm a large non-stick frying pan and add the coconut oil or butter. Place the slices of soaked bread in the pan and cook over a medium heat for about 2 minutes or until golden. Turn the slices over and cook on the other side.

4 Top the French toast with a heap of berries, then add a big dollop of Greek yoghurt and an extra drizzle of syrup if you like.

If you happen to love a chilli kick at any time of the day like I do, try my version of huevos rancheros (rancher's eggs). Of course the chillies are totally optional but I recommend the chorizo, as it adds an amazing smoky flavour to this hearty breakfast. For an extra treat, scatter over 50g of grated Mexicana cheese if you like. SERVES 4

Mexican Eggs

50g chorizo, cubed
1 red onion, finely diced
1/2 red chilli, finely diced
   (optional)
2 garlic cloves, crushed
1 x 400g can of
   chopped tomatoes
150g cherry tomatoes,
   halved
1/2 tsp smoked paprika
100ml water
4 organic free-range eggs
2 tbsp chopped
   fresh coriander
pickled jalapeños,
   to serve (optional)

1 Place a frying pan over a medium heat and dry fry the cubes of chorizo for 1–2 minutes. Add the onion, chilli, if using, and garlic and continue to cook for a couple of minutes. Then add the chopped tomatoes, cherry tomatoes, paprika and water and cook over a medium heat, uncovered, for a further 5 minutes.

2 Make 4 wells in the sauce and crack an egg into each one. Cover the pan with a lid and cook the eggs for 8–10 minutes or until the whites are almost set. Scatter with some fresh coriander and pickled jalapeños, if using, and serve at once.

The sweetness that comes from a slow-roasted tomato is a thing of beauty and this is just the recipe to give a boost to those bland, tasteless tomatoes we often find in our supermarkets. Slow-roasting and the addition of a few herbs really intensifies the flavour and makes the humble tomato taste how I think it should. This is the perfect light recipe for those lazy Sunday mornings shared with family and friends. **SERVES 4**

Slow-roasted Tomato Bagels

8 large, ripe plum
   tomatoes, halved
1 tbsp olive oil
1 tbsp balsamic vinegar
2 garlic cloves, crushed
2–3 sprigs of fresh thyme,
   leaves picked
2 tbsp white wine vinegar
4 free-range eggs
2 wholemeal bagels, halved
fresh chives, to garnish
sea salt
black pepper

1 Preheat the oven to 160°C/140°C Fan/Gas 3.

2 Put the tomato halves in a bowl with the olive oil, vinegar, garlic and thyme leaves and season with salt and pepper. Toss the tomatoes until they are all well coated with the oil and seasonings, then scatter them on a baking tray, cut side up. Roast for 45–50 minutes.

3 When the tomatoes are nearly ready, bring a saucepan of water to a rolling boil and add the white wine vinegar. Whisk vigorously to create a swirling vortex, then crack the eggs, 1 at a time, into a ramekin, and gently add each egg to the water. Turn off the heat, then leave the eggs to cook for 3–4 minutes for runny yolks. Use a slotted spoon to remove the eggs from the water and drain them on some kitchen paper.

4 Meanwhile, toast the bagels. Top each half with some tomatoes, a poached egg and finish with some fresh chives and a grinding of black pepper.

I love a full English as much as the next man, but having to use every pot and pan in the house when cooking it drives me crazy! This one-pan frittata is a favourite in my household and includes all the ingredients that make the full English such a classic but without the kitchen looking like a whirlwind has hit it! What's not to love? **SERVES 4**

Big Breakfast Frittata

1 tsp coconut oil
2 sausages (minimum
   80% pork)
8 free-range eggs
150g mushrooms, sliced
   (portobello are good)
4 rashers of lean, smoked
   bacon, trimmed of fat,
100g sunblush tomatoes
small handful of chives,
   sliced
sea salt
black pepper

1 Preheat the oven to 200°C/180°C Fan/Gas 6.

2 You need a large ovenproof frying pan. Heat a dash of oil in the pan and fry the sausages until cooked through. Remove the sausages from the pan and slice each one on the diagonal into 4 pieces, then set aside. Beat the eggs in a bowl and season with salt and black pepper.

3 In the same pan, cook the mushrooms and bacon over a medium-high heat. Put the pieces of sausage back in the pan and add the sunblush tomatoes, then pour in the eggs. Cook until the eggs have just set around the edges.

4 Transfer the pan to the preheated oven and cook the frittata for 6–8 minutes. Turn it out on to a plate, scatter with chives, then serve with a big dollop of your favourite sauce.

This recipe proves you don't need a list of ingredients as long as your arm to make something light, quick and delicious for breakfast. If you're not a fan of smoked salmon, this also works brilliantly with ham. SERVES 4

Baked Eggs with Salmon

100g baby spinach leaves
100g smoked salmon
4 free-range eggs
30g Parmesan
   cheese, grated
black pepper

1 Preheat the oven to 180°C/160°C Fan/Gas 4. Wash the spinach, then pile it into a large pan and place the pan on the heat until the leaves have wilted. Drain the spinach in a colander, then squeeze out as much water as you can. Set aside.

2 Take 4 ramekins and divide the cooked spinach and smoked salmon between them. Crack an egg into each one, being careful not to break the yolk. Top with some grated Parmesan and a grinding of black pepper.

3 Place the ramekins in a baking tray or roasting tin. Pour in just-boiled water to come halfway up the sides of the ramekins. Bake in the oven for 8–10 minutes or until the whites of the eggs are set. Serve at once.

Eggs are a brilliant standby for a quick and easy breakfast. They keep you feeling full for ages so help you avoid snacking between meals. The trick with scrambled eggs is to use a non-stick pan and to remove the pan from the heat before you think the eggs are done. They'll finish cooking in the hot pan. This dish can be cooked and served in under five minutes – I've timed it! SERVES 4

Masala Scrambled Eggs

1 tsp coconut oil
2 garlic cloves, crushed
1/2 green chilli, deseeded
    and finely diced (optional)
1/2 tsp garam masala
2 wholemeal bagels, halved
8 free-range eggs
2 tsp chopped fresh
    coriander, plus
    extra to serve
sea salt
black pepper

1 Warm a dash of oil in a small saucepan and fry the garlic and chilli, if using, for a minute. Add the garam masala and continue to cook for a further 30 seconds. Toast the bagel halves.

2 Meanwhile, beat the eggs in a bowl and season with salt and pepper. Add the eggs to the pan and cook over a medium heat, stirring as you go. When the eggs are almost done, remove the pan from the heat, stir in the coriander and let the residual heat in the saucepan finish the cooking of the eggs.

3 Serve the eggs on top of the toasted bagel halves and garnish with a little more coriander.

A cooked breakfast at the weekend is a real treat. It's often thought of as unhealthy but it doesn't have to be. By trimming the fat from the bacon, grilling rather than frying, and making my fabulous baked beans instead of using the sugar-laden shop-bought versions, you can make this delicious breakfast a guilt-free treat! Passata is simply uncooked sieved tomatoes and is available in jars in the supermarket. **SERVES 4**

Sunday Brekkie

1 tbsp coconut oil
4 large portobello
    mushrooms
4 large plum
    tomatoes, halved
3 sprigs of fresh thyme
8 rashers of rindless
    back bacon
splash of white wine vinegar
4 free-range eggs
sea salt
black pepper

Home-made baked beans
1 x 400g can of haricot beans
2 garlic cloves, crushed
1/2 tsp coconut oil
250ml tomato passata
100ml chicken stock
1 tbsp Worcestershire sauce
1/2 tsp smoked paprika
1 tsp brown sugar

1 Start by preparing the beans. Tip the beans into a saucepan, add the garlic and coconut oil and cook gently for 2–3 minutes before adding the rest of the ingredients (everything except the seasoning). Bring everything to a simmer and continue to cook for 10–15 minutes until the liquid has reduced, then season with salt and loads of black pepper.

2 Preheat the oven to 200°C/180°C Fan/Gas 6. Gently warm the coconut oil until melted. Place the mushrooms and tomatoes on a baking tray, drizzle them with the coconut oil and sprinkle with thyme, salt and pepper. Pop the tray into the oven and cook the mushrooms and tomatoes for 15–20 minutes.

3 When the beans, mushrooms and tomatoes are nearly ready, cook the bacon under a medium-hot grill for 2–3 minutes on each side until crispy.

4 Bring a saucepan of water to a rolling boil and add a splash of white wine vinegar. Whisk vigorously to create a swirling vortex, then crack the eggs, 1 at a time, into a ramekin, and gently add each egg to the water. Turn off the heat and leave the eggs to cook for 3–4 minutes for runny yolks. Use a slotted spoon to remove the eggs from the water and drain them on some kitchen paper. Serve at once with the rest of your delicious breakfast.

Refreshing juices will kick-start your system and also help towards your five a day. You can make them in a juicer or a blender, though you may have to add extra liquid if using a blender to get the right consistency. You won't believe how naturally sweet vegetables are, so start your kids on this green juice – and the beetroot juice on page 32 too. They'll love them. **SERVES 2**

Green Goodness Juice

1 Braeburn apple
1 pear
4 large handfuls
   of spinach or kale
2 celery stalks
1/2 cucumber
juice of 1 lime
8 fresh mint leaves
400ml coconut water or
   water (if using a blender)

1 Wash the apple, pear, spinach or kale, celery and cucumber. Pass them through a vegetable juicer, starting with the more fibrous vegetables first and finishing with the ones with a higher water content, such as the cucumber. Add the fresh lime juice and mint leaves and drink immediately over ice or within 24 hours.

2 If using a blender, place the apple, pear, spinach or kale, celery and cucumber with the liquid, then blitz until smooth. Add more liquid if required to get your desired consistency. Then add the lime juice and mint leaves and enjoy.

I have a massive passion for juicing. It's a fantastic way to get loads of vitamins and nutrients into my system and gives me a great energy boost. The juice only stays fresh for 24 hours so it's best to drink it straight away if you can. As a general rule, try to keep your juices vegetable heavy and only add one or two pieces of fruit. Use a blender with some additional liquid if you like, but a juicer is best with this one.   SERVES 2

Beetroot and Ginger Juice

2 beetroots
1 red pepper
3 handfuls of kale
3 carrots
1 Braeburn apple
1cm slice of fresh
   root ginger
$1/2$ cucumber
juice of $1/2$ lemon
up to 400ml coconut
   water or water
   (if using a blender)

1 Wash all the veg and fruit, then pass them through a vegetable juicer starting with the more fibrous vegetables first and finishing with the ones with a higher water content, such as cucumber. Add the lemon juice and drink immediately over ice or within 24 hours.

2 If using a blender, put the ingredients in the blender and blitz until smooth. Add coconut water or water as required to get the consistency you like.

Whenever I'm in a rush in the mornings, this is my breakfast of choice. I blitz it up, pour it into a travel cup and I'm out the door, carrying my smoothie with me. It really ticks all the boxes for me – contains loads of goodness, plus slow-release carbs to fuel the day, and best of all it tastes amazing. If using fresh fruit instead of frozen berries, throw in a couple of ice cubes while blending. **SERVES 2**

Superfood Protein Smoothie

1 banana
a handful of blueberries
500ml almond milk or
   skimmed milk
2 tbsp Greek yoghurt
a handful of frozen berries,
   such as raspberries,
   blackberries, strawberries
1 tbsp peanut butter
1 tbsp chia seeds (optional)
3 tbsp rolled oats
   (not jumbo)

1 Place all the ingredients in a blender and blitz until nice and smooth. Add a little more milk or water if necessary to get the consistency you like. Drink as soon as possible.

It might seem surprising, but try popping an avocado into your breakfast smoothie. Avocados are packed full of vitamins and nutrients and will set you up for the day ahead. I like this smoothie as it is, but if you like yours a little sweeter, add a little honey to taste. SERVES 2

Avocado and Banana Smoothie

2 handfuls of baby spinach
1 ripe avocado
2 bananas, peeled
1 tsp chia seeds (optional)
400ml unsweetened
   almond milk
handful of ice cubes

1 Put all the ingredients into a blender and blitz until lovely and smooth.

2 If necessary, add a little extra almond milk or water to get the consistency you like.

CHAPTER 2

LUNCH

The key to a successful lunch is planning. If you don't plan and prepare ahead, you and your family are likely to end up eating something you shouldn't – perhaps temptingly packaged but full of preservatives. That was how I used to live. Lunch was a trip to the café or the shops to buy a limp sandwich, a bag of crisps, chocolate and a can of fizzy drink. Yes, I'm ashamed to say that was my diet! And eating like this wasn't cheap. Before I changed my ways, I'd spend around £6 a day on lunch. Times that by five and it's £30 a week, then multiply it by 52 and you've spent a whopping £1,560 a year. If you're feeding a family of four that's a lot of money. Imagine all the fresh ingredients you could buy for that sum!

My suggestions for healthy, delicious lunches will cost you a bit in time, but many can be prepared in advance or put together quickly – give my avocado and prawn toasts or the courgette salad a try. Make them the evening before or in the morning and if you're going to be on the move, box them up but keep the dressings separate until you're ready to eat. The secret is to think ahead. If you fail to prepare for healthy eating, then prepare to fail!

There's nothing more comforting than a hearty, silky smooth soup. This recipe is inspired by my love of Caribbean food and has the perfect balance of sweetness and mild spicing. The quinoa (pronounced KEEN-WA) is fairly plain, like couscous, so you need to bring flavour to it with spices and a little chilli if you like. Quinoa is a great way of adding protein to this veggie soup, though, so do give it a go. SERVES 4

Sunshine Butternut Soup

1 butternut squash, diced
1 large carrot, diced
1 large onion, diced
3 garlic cloves, chopped
1/2 red chilli, deseeded
   (optional)
3 sprigs of fresh thyme
1 tbsp grated fresh
   root ginger
1 tsp coconut oil
1/2 tsp ground cinnamon
1/2 tsp ground allspice
100g quinoa
700ml vegetable stock
juice of 1 lime
chopped fresh coriander,
   to serve
sea salt
black pepper

1 Place the butternut squash, carrot, onion, garlic, chilli, if using, thyme and ginger in a large saucepan along with the coconut oil. Cook gently for 10 minutes until the vegetables have softened slightly, then add the spices and cook for a further minute.

2 Rinse the quinoa well in water and add it to the pan with the stock. Bring the soup to the boil, then cover the pan with a lid and simmer over a low heat for about 30 minutes.

3 Leave the soup to cool slightly, then blitz to a smooth consistency with a hand blender or in a food processor. Season with salt, pepper and a good squeeze of lime juice, then garnish each bowlful with chopped coriander before serving.

Jars of roasted red peppers are a great store-cupboard standby. You can buy them in supermarkets and they save you the time-consuming task of cooking peppers over a flame or hot grill and peeling them. What's more, if you think how much it costs to buy five or six peppers to roast yourself you realize that these jars are excellent value for money. **SERVES 4**

Roasted Red Pepper Gazpacho

½ cucumber, peeled
  and deseeded
200g roasted red peppers
  (drained weight),
  finely diced
1 green pepper, finely diced
1 small red onion, diced
600g ripe plum tomatoes
1 large garlic clove
60g ciabatta bread,
  cut into cubes
1 x 500g carton of
  tomato passata
3 tbsp extra virgin olive
  oil, plus extra to serve
2 tbsp sherry vinegar
Tabasco, to taste (optional)
8 black olives, stoned
  and quartered
sea salt
black pepper

1 Peel the cucumber and cut it into quarters. Using a sharp knife, cut out the seeds out of each quarter and discard them. It's important to do this, as the cucumber seeds make the soup too watery.

2 Set aside some of the peppers and onion to garnish the soup. Place the rest with the plum tomatoes, cucumber, garlic, ciabatta and tomato passata in a blender or food processor and blitz until smooth.

3 Pour the soup into a large bowl and add the oil and vinegar, then season with the Tabasco, if using, and salt and pepper. If you have time, leave the soup at room temperature for 30 minutes to let the flavours develop.

4 Serve the soup garnished with the reserved diced peppers and onion, black olives and another drizzle of olive oil.

Here's another good soup recipe using roasted red peppers. I like to make a large pot of soup and, if we don't need it all right away, I divide it into portions and pop them in the freezer to enjoy another time. SERVES 4

Roasted Red Pepper and Avocado Soup

1 tsp coconut oil
600g ripe tomatoes
    (about 6 tomatoes)
250g baby plum tomatoes
2 onions, roughly diced
2 garlic cloves, crushed
1 tsp ground cumin
600ml vegetable stock
300g roasted red peppers
    from a jar, roughly
    chopped
juice of $\frac{1}{2}$ lime
small bunch of coriander,
    roughly chopped
30ml olive oil
1 avocado, flesh diced
sea salt
black pepper

1 Melt the coconut oil in a large saucepan. Add the tomatoes, onions and garlic and cook over a low to medium heat for 10 minutes, then sprinkle in the cumin. Add the stock and peppers, then simmer for another 5 minutes.

2 Pour the soup into a blender and blitz until smooth. Season with salt and pepper, then add in a good squeeze of lime juice.

3 Put most of the coriander and the olive oil in a small blender and blitz. Drizzle each bowl of soup with some of this oil and garnish with the remaining chopped coriander and the diced avocado.

Turkey is an underused meat in my opinion. It's easy to cook with, it's lean and best of all it's cheap. Try to find a naturally brewed soy sauce – several brands on the market are artificially produced so always read the label before buying. This recipe is really tasty as well as simple and quick, which makes it a winner for me and great for a light lunch. **SERVES 4**

Fragrant Turkey Noodle Broth

1 litre of good chicken stock
3 garlic cloves, crushed
1 tbsp grated fresh
    root ginger
1 red chilli, sliced (optional)
500g lean turkey breast,
    thinly sliced
100g bean sprouts
4 or 5 spring onions, sliced
1–2 tbsp soy sauce, to taste
4 egg noodle nests
small bunch of fresh mint,
    chopped, to serve
small bunch of fresh
    coriander, chopped,
    to serve

1 Pour the stock into a large saucepan and bring it to a simmer. Add the garlic, ginger and chilli, if using, and cook for 5 minutes. Add the sliced turkey and continue cooking for 10 minutes before stirring in the bean sprouts and some of the sliced spring onions. Season with soy sauce to taste.

2 Meanwhile, cook the noodles in boiling water for 3–4 minutes. Drain well and serve 1 nest into each bowl, then ladle in the broth. Finish the dish with the rest of the spring onions and plenty of mint and coriander.

My daughter Indie has a taste for a certain brand of cream of tomato soup and I was shocked to find out how much added sugar it contains – not surprising she likes it so much. So I set about creating a naturally sweet tomato soup for her, which she enjoys, although I have to serve hers before I blitz it with the basil. Can't win them all, eh? That's kids for you but I'm working on it! **SERVES 4**

Roasted Tomato and Basil Soup

6 ripe tomatoes, halved
200g baby plum
   tomatoes, halved
1 tsp coconut oil
2 carrots, diced
2 onions, diced
2 celery sticks, diced
3 garlic cloves, crushed
600ml vegetable stock
small bunch of fresh basil,
   plus extra to serve
1 heaped tbsp Greek yoghurt
sea salt
black pepper

1 Preheat the oven to 180°C/160° Fan/Gas 4. Place all the tomatoes on a baking tray and roast them for about 40 minutes.

2 Meanwhile, heat the oil in a saucepan, add the carrots, onions, celery and garlic and cook them gently for 10 minutes. Don't allow them to colour.

3 When the tomatoes are ready, tip them into the saucepan, add the stock and simmer for 10 minutes. Transfer the soup to a blender, add the basil and blitz until smooth. Add the yoghurt and pulse until it's all incorporated. Season the soup with salt and pepper to taste and serve with some more fresh basil.

Avocados are a staple in my diet, full of good fats and surprisingly high in protein for a fruit! And here's a quick tip – if your avocados are under-ripe put them in a bowl with some bananas and they ripen up fast. Avocados are rarely cooked but believe me they are amazing baked. Use the tortillas to scoop out the yummy filling for a great light lunch. **SERVES 4**

Baked Avocado with Eggs and Baked Tortilla Chips

2 avocados, halved
  and stones removed
4 small free-range eggs
2 small flour tortillas,
  cut into triangles
100g smoked pancetta
  lardons
1/2 tsp red chilli flakes
  (optional)
chopped fresh coriander,
  to garnish
sea salt

1 Preheat the oven to 180°C/160°C Fan/Gas 4. Put the avocado halves on a baking tray, placing them on some scrunched-up foil to keep them level. Carefully crack an egg into each pit – you might not fit in all of the egg white, but don't worry. Bake the avocados for 18–20 minutes or until the whites are set and the yolks are cooked to your liking.

2 Put the tortilla triangles on a baking tray and 5 minutes before the avocados are due to be ready, pop the tortilla chips into the oven to crisp up.

3 Meanwhile, fry the pancetta in a dry pan until golden and crispy. Remove the avocados and chips from the oven and scatter over the pancetta, some chilli flakes, if using, and a little sea salt if you like. Garnish with some fresh coriander and serve at once.

The flavour combinations in this recipe are some of my favourites and the roasted beetroot with its sticky balsamic glaze works perfectly with the creamy horseradish dressing. The beets are great hot or cold so if you like you can cook them the night before so you can put the salad together in no time the next day. Use golden or regular beets – or both! **SERVES 4**

Sticky Baked Beetroot Salad

6 beetroots, peeled
   and quartered
1 tsp olive oil
1 tbsp balsamic vinegar
3–4 sprigs of fresh thyme
400g smoked salmon
1/2 red onion, thinly sliced
6 radishes, thinly sliced
4 handfuls of salad leaves,
   such as baby watercress
   or lamb's lettuce
lemon wedges, to serve
sea salt
black pepper

Dressing
100ml low-fat
   natural yoghurt
1 heaped tsp
   horseradish sauce
juice of 1/2 lemon
2 tbsp chopped dill

1 Preheat the oven to 190°C/170° Fan/Gas 5. Put the beetroot quarters in a bowl, dress them with the oil, balsamic vinegar and thyme, then season with a little salt and pepper. Tip the dressed beetroots on to a large sheet of foil and scrunch up the edges to make a parcel. Pop this on a baking tray and roast in the preheated oven for an hour. Set aside to cool slightly.

2 Whisk the dressing ingredients together in a small bowl, then set aside. Divide the beetroot quarters, salmon, onion, radish slices and leaves between 4 plates, then drizzle over some of the dressing. Serve with the rest of the dressing and lemon wedges.

I love this fresh salad. It makes the most of beautiful summer courgettes and can be put together in minutes. It's also perfect as a packed lunch to take to work. Just serve some into a container and take along a small jar of dressing. Shake up the dressing, add it to your salad and your lunch is ready. **SERVES 4**

Courgette and Feta Salad

3 courgettes
200g frozen peas, defrosted
3–4 spring onions, sliced
8 radishes, thinly sliced
small handful of fresh
    mint, leaves picked
    from the stems
1 heaped tsp coconut oil
2 slices of wholemeal
    bread, cut into cubes
80g feta cheese, crumbled

Dressing
1 tbsp sherry vinegar
2 tbsp olive oil
1/2 tsp honey
1/2 tsp Dijon mustard
1/2 garlic clove, crushed
sea salt
black pepper

1 Using a vegetable peeler, cut the courgettes into ribbons. Put these in a bowl with the peas, spring onions, radishes and mint leaves.

2 Heat the oil in a pan over a medium heat, then add the cubes of bread and cook them until golden. Remove the cubes and leave them to drain on some kitchen paper.

3 Whisk the dressing ingredients in a small jug and season with salt and pepper. Dress the vegetables, then add the cubes of bread and crumble the feta cheese on top.

I can't resist the flavours of India. Luckily, not all Indian food is laden with the large amounts of ghee found in the average takeaway and there are loads of healthy choices. Do try to marinate the chicken for this salad overnight, as the flavours will be incredible – planning ahead is the key! If you're being extra strict with yourself, leave out the croutons – but they are good! SERVES 4

Chicken Tikka Salad with Naan Croutons

50ml low-fat natural yoghurt
2 tbsp tikka masala paste
3 garlic cloves, crushed
1 tbsp grated fresh
　root ginger
1 tsp garam masala
$1/2$ tsp turmeric
juice of $1/2$ lemon
4 chicken breasts,
　skin removed
1 small naan bread,
　cut into cubes
1 tbsp olive oil
4 handfuls of mixed
　salad leaves
4 handfuls of baby spinach
$1/2$ red onion, sliced
　(optional)
small bunch of fresh
　coriander, chopped,
　to serve

Cucumber Dressing
$1/2$ cucumber, peeled,
　deseeded and diced
100ml low-fat
　natural yoghurt
3 tbsp chopped fresh mint
$1/2$ tsp ground cumin
juice of $1/2$ lemon

1 Mix the yoghurt, tikka masala paste, garlic, ginger, garam masala, turmeric and lemon juice in a large bowl. Add the chicken breasts and leave them to marinate for a couple of hours or overnight if possible.

2 Cut the marinated chicken breasts into chunks and thread them on to soaked wooden skewers. Preheat a griddle pan or a barbecue and cook the chicken for 7–8 minutes on each side or until cooked through.

3 Meanwhile, preheat the oven to 200°C/180°C Fan/ Gas 6. Put the cubes of bread in a bowl with the olive oil and turn them so they are all well coated. Tip them on to a baking tray and cook for 8–10 minutes in the preheated oven.

4 To make the dressing, mix the cucumber, yoghurt, mint, cumin and lemon juice in a bowl. Set aside for 5 minutes to allow the flavours to develop.

5 To serve, put some salad leaves, baby spinach and onion, if using, in each bowl. Add the chicken tikka and croutons on top, then drizzle over the cucumber dressing. Garnish with fresh coriander.

I first started making this dish a few years ago after eating something similar in a local restaurant. I know chorizo is a little fatty but it adds a touch of luxury and lots of flavour. The chickpeas bulk out this recipe to make it more substantial but feel free to omit them if you want something lighter. I have to confess that I've been very selfish in this book and used lots of raw red onion in salads, as I'm a big fan. If your kids find the flavour too harsh, you can leave the onion out – the salad will still be amazing! **SERVES 4**

Chicken and Chorizo Salad

2 chicken breasts,
   skinned and sliced
2 garlic cloves, crushed
3–4 sprigs of fresh thyme
1/2 tsp smoked paprika
1 tsp olive oil
50g chorizo, thinly sliced
1 x 400g can of chickpeas
4 handfuls of baby spinach
1 red onion, thinly sliced
   (optional)
80g sunblush tomatoes
sea salt
black pepper

Dressing
1/2 garlic clove, crushed
1 tsp sherry vinegar
1 tsp extra virgin olive oil
1 tsp wholegrain mustard

1 Put the slices of chicken in a resealable freezer bag and add the garlic, thyme, paprika and olive oil. Seal the bag and massage it well to make sure everything is thoroughly mixed, then leave the chicken to marinate for at least 1 hour.

2 Heat a dry frying pan, add the chorizo slices and cook them for 1–2 minutes on each side. Remove them from the pan and set aside to drain on kitchen paper. Tip the chickpeas into the pan and cook them for 2–3 minutes in the oil released by the chorizo, then season with a dash of salt and pepper.

3 Preheat a griddle pan. Remove the slices of chicken from the marinade and cook them for 2–3 minutes on each side or until cooked through.

4 Put the baby spinach in a large bowl and add the chickpeas, sliced onion, if using, and chorizo. Whisk together the dressing ingredients and pour the dressing over the salad, then top with the chicken and sunblush tomatoes.

Filo pastry is very low in fat compared to other kinds of pastry, but we often paint it with copious amounts of butter, and so bump up the calories and the fat! To help get my filo crisp I use just a light brushing of butter – you don't need a lot. The parcels are wonderful served with my Greek tomato salad and it's worth investing a couple of extra pennies to get some great-tasting tomatoes for a real flavour of Greece. **SERVES 4**

Spinach and Feta Filo Parcels with Greek Salad

1 tsp coconut oil
1 large onion, sliced
3 garlic cloves, crushed
500g baby spinach
100g feta cheese, crumbled
2 eggs, beaten
1 tsp dried oregano
small grating of nutmeg
juice of 1/2 lemon
6–8 sheets of filo pastry
20g unsalted butter, melted
sea salt
black pepper

Greek Salad
150g cherry tomatoes
60g feta cheese,
   cut into cubes
1/2 red onion, sliced
1/2 cucumber, deseeded
   and diced
80g black olives
1 tsp fresh oregano
   or 1/2 tsp dried
30ml olive oil
juice of 1/2 lemon

1 Heat the oil in a frying pan and cook the onion and garlic for about 5 minutes until softened. Put the spinach in a large saucepan, cover it with a lid and place over a gentle heat until wilted. Drain the spinach, squeeze out the excess water, then leave it to cool.

2 Chop the spinach roughly and put it in a bowl with the onion, garlic, feta, eggs, oregano, nutmeg and lemon juice. Mix everything together well and season with salt and pepper.

3 Preheat the oven to 180°C/160°C Fan/Gas 4. Take a sheet of filo, brush it lightly with melted butter, then fold it lengthways to make a long rectangle. Brush this with more butter, place a large spoonful of the spinach mixture on the bottom left-hand corner of the pastry. Fold the pastry from corner to corner until the mixture is fully enclosed. Repeat until you've used all the filo and filling.

4 Place the parcels on a greased baking tray and bake them for 20–25 minutes or until golden brown.

5 To make the salad, mix all the ingredients in a large bowl and leave to stand for 10 minutes for the flavours to blend. Serve the salad with the parcels.

Tortillas are great at any time of day. They're quick and easy to make and you can put in whatever vegetables, meat or cheese you have in the fridge. And if there's any tortilla left over it will taste even better the next day. I like to serve this with some sweet potato wedges. **SERVES 4**

Summer Asparagus Tortilla

2 small sweet potatoes,
    cut into wedges
1 tbsp olive oil
1 bunch of asparagus
1 tsp coconut oil
1 courgette, thinly sliced
2 garlic cloves, crushed
1 red onion, sliced
6 free-range eggs
sea salt
black pepper

1 Start with the sweet potato wedges. Preheat the oven to 200°C/180° Fan/Gas 6. Cook the wedges in a pan of boiling water for 5 minutes, then drain. Add the olive oil and mix so all the wedges are coated, then put them on a baking tray and season with salt and pepper. Bake for about 30 minutes.

2 Meanwhile, bring a pan of salted water to the boil. Add the asparagus, bring the water back to the boil then cook for 2–3 minutes. Drain the asparagus, then set it aside.

3 Heat the coconut oil in a non-stick, ovenproof pan, add the sliced courgette and garlic and fry them until golden – this will take 6–7 minutes. Add the sliced onion to the pan and continue to cook until the onion has softened.

4 Beat the eggs in a bowl and season with salt and pepper. Add the asparagus to the frying pan with the other veg, then pour in the seasoned beaten eggs and cook until the eggs have just set around the edges. Pop the pan in the hot oven with the sweet potato wedges for 6–8 minutes until cooked through.

5 Remove the pan from the oven – remember it will be very hot. Place a plate over the pan and carefully invert the pan to turn the tortilla on to the plate. Cut the tortilla into slices and serve with the sweet potato wedges. By the way, if you don't have a pan that can go in the oven, finish the tortilla under a medium-hot grill for a few minutes until the eggs have set and the top is golden.

These open sandwiches definitely pack a punch in the flavour department. I love making salsas and guacamole and always make more than I need so I have some left over for the next day. Salsa, or sauce, is great with so many meals but many supermarket varieties are packed full of sugar and taste nowhere near as good as this one. Please give it a go. **SERVES 4**

Avocado and Garlic Prawn Toasts

1 tsp coconut oil
400g shelled raw prawns
$\frac{1}{2}$ red chilli, very finely diced (optional)
2 garlic cloves, crushed
juice of $\frac{1}{2}$ lime
4 thin slices of wholemeal or sourdough bread
chopped fresh coriander, to serve
lime wedges, to serve
sea salt
black pepper

Guacamole
2 ripe avocados
$\frac{1}{2}$ red onion, very finely diced
1 garlic clove, crushed
$\frac{1}{2}$ red chilli, very finely diced (optional)
juice of 1 lime
2 tbsp fresh coriander

Salsa
100g baby plum tomatoes
150g roasted red peppers (from a jar)
$\frac{1}{2}$ red onion, finely diced
2 tbsp chopped fresh coriander
juice of 1 lime
30ml olive oil

1 First make the guacamole. Cut the avocados in half, remove the stones and scoop the flesh into a bowl. Mash the avocado, then stir in the onion, garlic and chilli, if using. Add the lime juice and chopped coriander and season with salt and pepper, then cover the bowl with cling film and set aside.

2 To make the salsa, finely chop the tomatoes, peppers and onion, place them all in a bowl, then add the coriander. Season, then dress with the lime juice and olive oil.

3 Heat the coconut oil in a pan, add the shelled prawns and cook them for 1–2 minutes on each side until pink. Throw in the chilli, if using, and the garlic, then cook for a further 30 seconds. Add the lime juice and season with salt and pepper.

4 Toast the slices of bread and spread them with guacamole. Add some prawns, sprinkle salsa on top, then garnish with fresh coriander and serve with wedges of lime on the side.

This is such a simple recipe – just a few ingredients but so tasty, like all Italian food! It's perfect for showcasing great seasonal produce such as courgettes and you can use other vegetables such as aubergines, spring onions or asparagus. It's great-tasting fuel for the body and a perfect lunch for me if I'm training later on in the day, but I find that little ones love it too – not that they usually need any more energy! It's me that needs extra when I'm running around after my little one! **SERVES 4**

Griddled Courgette and Gremolata Pasta

16 baby courgettes, sliced
    in half lengthways
1 tbsp olive oil
200g wholewheat pasta
    (such as fusilli)
sea salt
black pepper

Gremolata
20g freshly grated
    wholegrain breadcrumbs
juice of 1/2 lemon
zest of 1 unwaxed lemon
1 garlic clove, crushed
2 tbsp very finely chopped
    flat-leaf parsley

1 Place the courgettes in a bowl, drizzle them with the oil, then season with salt and pepper. Get a griddle pan lovely and hot and cook the courgettes for 2–3 minutes on each side.

2 To make the gremolata, toast the breadcrumbs in a dry frying pan until golden. Mix them with the lemon juice, zest, garlic and parsley and season lightly with salt and pepper.

3 Cook the pasta in lots of boiling, salted water according to the packet instructions. Drain the pasta, then stir in the griddled courgettes and the gremolata. Serve at once.

If you're after a quick and simple lunch, this is the recipe for you. I love cashew nuts, and their creamy texture adds so much to this punchy pesto. Double up on the pesto recipe and keep the rest in a bowl under a thin layer of oil for a day or two, ready to go when you are. I like to grate over a little more Parmesan cheese before eating my helping. SERVES 4

Cashew Nut Pesto Pasta

200g baby plum
  tomatoes, halved
2 garlic cloves, crushed
1 tbsp olive oil
240g wholewheat linguine
8 slices of smoked pancetta
  (about 80g)
grated Parmesan cheese
  (optional)
sea salt
black pepper

Cashew pesto
large bunch of fresh basil
40g cashew nuts
1/2 garlic clove
lemon juice to taste
50ml extra virgin olive oil

1 Preheat the oven to 150°C/130°C Fan/Gas 2. Place the halved tomatoes on a baking tray, scatter the garlic over them, then drizzle with the oil. Season the tomatoes with salt and pepper and roast them for about 30 minutes. Remove and set aside. (Or, if you're very short of time, you can use 100g of sunblush tomatoes instead.)

2 To make the pesto, put the basil in a blender with the cashews, garlic, lemon juice and oil, then blitz to a loose consistency. Season to taste with salt and pepper.

3 Bring a large pan of salted water to the boil and cook the pasta for 10–12 minutes or according to the instructions on the packet.

4 Cook the pancetta under a medium hot grill for 1–2 minutes on each side or until golden and crisp.

5 Drain the pasta and stir in the pesto and tomatoes. Break up the pancetta slices, scatter them over the top and serve at once – with grated Parmesan if you like.

These fishcakes are fragrant and delicious – and dead simple to make. I find a mini food processor is a great piece of kit to have in the kitchen. It makes easy work of breaking down the fish for this recipe and can be used for making quick pastes, pestos and dips, saving you the effort of lugging that massive processor out of the cupboard. Serve these with salad or with some rice or noodles to make a lovely lunch for the family.

SERVES 4

Thai Fishcakes with Mango Salsa

200g salmon fillet, skinned and roughly cubed
170g can of crabmeat chunks, drained
1 tbsp grated fresh root ginger
2 tbsp fresh coriander, chopped
1 tsp Thai red curry paste
1 egg, beaten
juice of 1 lime
50g green beans, finely sliced
1 tbsp coconut oil
sea salt
black pepper

Mango salsa
1 mango, peeled and diced
1/2 red onion finely diced
2 tbsp fresh coriander, chopped
1/2 red chilli finely diced (optional)
juice 1/2 lime
1 tbsp olive oil

1 Place all the fishcake ingredients, except the beans, coconut oil and seasoning, in a blender or food processor and pulse until the fish is broken down.

2 Tip the mixture into a bowl, season with salt and pepper and stir in the beans. Divide the mixture into golf ball-sized pieces and place them on a plate, flattening them out a little as you do so. Chill the fishcakes in the fridge for 20 minutes.

3 While the fishcakes are chilling, make the salsa. Mix the diced mango, onion, coriander and chilli, if using, then add the lime juice and olive oil. Season with salt and pepper.

4 Heat the coconut oil in a frying pan. Fry the fishcakes for 2–3 minutes on each side or until golden. Serve with the salsa and some salad leaves or rice and noodles.

CHAPTER 3
SPEEDY SUPPERS

I reckon that part of the reason why processed ready meals have become such a firm fixture in many family kitchens is that lots of us think we don't have time to cook up a fresh tasty meal. The temptation when you're in a rush is to grab a supermarket cottage pie and some frozen veg, then top it all off with gravy made from instant granules, but I suspect that anything that sits on a shelf for weeks or even months can't be that great for you, can it?

I firmly believe that fresh food is best for me and my family and I've realized that good tasty meals don't always have to be time-consuming to make. This chapter of speedy suppers ticks all the boxes for me, so please give my sweet potato rösti or Goan fish curry a whirl. You'll be amazed at how quickly you can have supper on the table.

Warming and fragrant, kedgeree is so simple to make. It's traditionally served for brunch, but I love it at any time of day. Most recipes include smoked haddock but I like to use salmon. For a real time-saver, though, try smoked salmon instead of fresh and simply stir it in to heat through gently before serving with soft-centred boiled eggs. **SERVES 4**

Fragrant Cauliflower Kedgeree

2 tsp coconut oil
400g salmon fillets, skinned
1 onion, very finely diced
1 large cauliflower, grated
1 tsp ground cumin
1 tsp ground coriander
1 tsp mustard seeds
1/2 tsp turmeric
1 green chilli, deseeded and
  finely chopped (optional)
6 spring onions, finely sliced
2 tbsp chopped
  fresh coriander
1 1/2 lemons
4 free-range eggs
sea salt
black pepper

1 Heat a teaspoon of the coconut oil in a frying pan, add the salmon fillets and cook them for 3–4 minutes over a medium to high heat until you can see that the fish is done three-quarters of the way through. Flip the fillets over, turn off the heat and leave them in the pan for 2–3 minutes to finish cooking.

2 Heat the remaining coconut oil in a separate pan and fry the diced onion for 5 minutes until softened. Add the grated cauliflower and continue cooking for 3–4 minutes, then add the spices and chilli, if using and cook for a further minute. Flake the cooked salmon into the pan and add the spring onions and some of the coriander. Season with salt and pepper and a good squeeze of lemon juice.

3 Meanwhile, put the eggs in a small pan of water, bring to the boil and cook for 7 minutes for medium runny yolks. Leave the eggs to cool slightly, then peel off their shells and cut them into quarters. Serve the kedgeree garnished with egg quarters, lemon wedges and chopped coriander.

Röstis were all the rage in the nineties. I don't think I ever saw an episode of 'Ready Steady Cook' that didn't feature a chef making one. And there was a good reason for this – röstis taste wonderful! This simple supper relies on just a few quality ingredients. You'll need to divide the mixture between two frying pans, as you don't want the rösti to be too thick.

SERVES 4

Sweet Potato Rösti with Chorizo and Eggs

2 large sweet
    potatoes, grated
1 large onion, thinly sliced
2 tbsp plain flour
2 tbsp fresh thyme, leaves
    picked from the stems
1 tsp smoked paprika
150g chorizo, cut into cubes
2 heaped tbsp coconut oil
4 free-range eggs
sea salt
black pepper

1 Grate the potato, then pile it on to a clean tea towel and squeeze out as much of the water as you can. Tip the grated potato into a bowl and add the onion, flour, some of the thyme leaves and the paprika. Mix well and season with salt and pepper.

2 Divide the cubes of chorizo between 2 frying pans and cook them for 1–2 minutes until they start to release their spicy oils.

3 Add a tablespoon of coconut oil to each pan, then divide the potato and onion mixture between the pans, spreading it in a thin layer. Cook over a medium heat until the mixture starts to brown, then break it up and leave to brown again. This will take about 8–10 minutes.

4 Preheat your grill to high. Make 2 wells in the rösti in each pan, then crack in the eggs. Continue cooking until the whites of the eggs are just starting to set, then place the pans under the hot grill and cook until the whites are set. Garnish with the rest of the fresh thyme and serve at once.

This tomato salad recipe comes from Tuscany, but during the summer months when British tomatoes are bang in season it makes numerous appearances on my supper table. The croutons soak up the sharp vinaigrette and add a beautiful texture to this colourful dish.

SERVES 4

Tomato and Mozzarella Panzanella Salad

8 large ripe plum tomatoes
1/2 cucumber, deseeded
   and diced
1/2 red onion, finely sliced
2 garlic cloves, crushed
3–4 sprigs of fresh thyme
2 tbsp extra virgin olive oil
1 tbsp red wine vinegar
1/2 loaf ciabatta bread
   (stale is good)
1 tbsp olive oil
4 handfuls of rocket leaves
1 ball of mozzarella,
   torn into pieces
bunch of fresh basil
sea salt
black pepper

1 Cut the tomatoes into quarters and put them in a large bowl with the diced cucumber, onion, garlic and thyme. Dress the salad with the extra virgin olive oil and vinegar, season with salt and pepper and then leave to stand for 30 minutes – the tomatoes must be at room temperature before eating.

2 Preheat the oven to 200°C/180° Fan/Gas 6. Cut or tear the ciabatta into chunks of about 2.5 centimetres and drizzle them with the tablespoon of olive oil. Scatter them on a baking tray and cook for about 10 minutes in the preheated oven.

3 Just before serving, add the ciabatta croutons and rocket leaves to the tomato salad and toss well. Serve the salad on plates or in bowls along with any juices, then top with pieces of mozzarella and basil leaves.

Tom yum soup is one of the lovely Lorraine Kelly's favourite dishes. I perfected this recipe as I thought it would score me a few brownie points when I cooked it for her on the show! In all honesty, it's one of my favourites too. I love the balance of hot, sweet and sour flavours and it just goes to show that food doesn't have to be loaded up with fat and salt to pack a flavour punch. You'll find scallops on the fish counter at your local supermarket or you can buy them frozen, although the texture of the fresh ones is better. **SERVES 4**

Salmon and Scallop Tom Yum Soup

1 thumb-sized piece of fresh root ginger (about 25g), peeled
1–2 red chillies, deseeded (optional), plus extra to serve
1 onion, roughly diced
4 garlic cloves
1 tbsp soy sauce
1 lemon grass stalk
1 tbsp coconut oil
1 litre of chicken stock
about 1 tbsp honey (or palm sugar if you can get it), to taste
200g oyster mushrooms, sliced
200g salmon fillet, skinned and diced into 1cm pieces
6 scallops, sliced in half horizontally
1–2 limes
fresh mint, to serve
6 spring onions, finely sliced, to serve

1 Place the ginger, chillies, if using, onion, garlic and soy sauce in a small blender and blitz to make a fine paste.

2 Give the lemon grass a good bash with a rolling pin to release its fragrant oils. Heat the coconut oil in a large saucepan over a medium heat, then add the lemon grass and the ginger paste and fry for 3–4 minutes. Pour in the stock and bring it to the boil, then add honey (or palm sugar) to taste. Reduce the heat to a simmer and cook for 10 minutes.

3 Add the mushrooms to the stock and cook them for 2–3 minutes, then add the salmon and scallops and cook for another 3–4 minutes. Squeeze in some lime juice to taste.

4 Ladle the soup into bowls, then garnish with fresh mint, sliced spring onions and some more chilli if you like it hot!

Some people are a little squeamish when it comes to squid, but it's great to eat so don't be put off. Your supermarket fishmonger will clean and prep it for you – job done. Squid must be cooked either very, very fast or nice and slowly. Anything in between and it will be rubbery. I'm a massive fan of quick and speedy recipes so I'm cooking this squid the fast way. **SERVES 4**

Speedy Griddled Squid Salad

4 small squid, cleaned
1 tbsp olive oil
60g cashew nuts
2 carrots, peeled
1 small cucumber
1 slightly under-ripe mango, peeled and cut into matchstick strips
100g beansprouts
small handful of fresh mint
small handful of fresh basil
1/2 red chilli, sliced (optional)
black pepper

Dressing
1/2 red chilli, deseeded and finely diced (optional)
1 garlic clove, crushed
1 tsp grated fresh root ginger
1 tbsp soy sauce
2 tbsp olive oil
juice of 1 lime
1 tbsp honey

1 Whisk all the dressing ingredients together in a small bowl and set aside.

2 Cut open the tube-like bodies of the squid. Using a sharp knife, score the outside of the body in a criss-cross pattern, being careful not to cut all the way through the flesh. Place the pieces of squid, and the tentacles too, in a bowl with a tablespoon of olive oil and some of the dressing and leave to marinate for no longer than 5 minutes. Lightly toast the cashews in a dry pan and set aside.

3 Heat a non-stick pan on the hob. Place the squid, scored-side down, in the pan with the tentacles and cook for 2–3 minutes. Remove the pieces of squid from the pan and cut them into bite-sized pieces.

4 Using a vegetable peeler, peel ribbons of carrot and cucumber and place them in a salad bowl with the mango and beansprouts. Pour the rest of the dressing over the salad and toss well.

5 Serve the salad with the cooked squid and garnish with the mint, basil, toasted cashews and some sliced chilli, if using. Season with pepper and serve at once.

I make my version of this classic French salad with juicy pink fresh tuna steaks. You can, of course, use good-quality tinned tuna but it won't have quite the same beautiful texture and flavour as the griddled fresh fish. If you're lucky enough to be basking in hot sunshine, oil the tuna and bang it on a barbecue for a couple of minutes on each side. SERVES 4

Tuna Steak Niçoise Salad

200g green beans
4 free-range eggs
4 small, fresh tuna steaks
3 little gem lettuces
6 plum tomatoes, quartered
50g black olives, pitted
sea salt
black pepper

Dressing
30ml extra virgin olive oil
1 tbsp sherry vinegar
1/2 tsp Dijon mustard
1/2 garlic clove, crushed

1 Cook the green beans in a pan of boiling, salted water for 4–5 minutes, then drain them, plunge them into a bowl of ice water and drain again.

2 Put the eggs in a small pan of water, bring them to the boil and cook for 7 minutes. Leave the eggs to cool slightly, then peel off the shells and cut the eggs into quarters.

3 Preheat a cast-iron griddle or a heavy-based frying pan. Season the tuna steaks with salt and pepper, add them to the hot pan and cook them for 2–3 minutes on each side. This will leave the fish slightly pink in the centre so if you prefer your tuna cooked through, cook it a little longer.

4 Meanwhile, make the dressing by whisking together the oil, vinegar, mustard and garlic, then season with salt and pepper.

5 Put the lettuce leaves and green beans in a large bowl and toss them with the dressing. Serve on to 4 plates, then add the tomatoes, eggs and a scattering of olives and top with the tuna.

This is a dead simple recipe that's packed full of flavour. Salmon is a particularly nutritious fish, full of protein and omega-3 fatty acids. I love using baby pak choi when I can find it, but stir-fried seasonal greens also work well in this dish. For a more substantial meal, serve the salmon with some noodles. SERVES 4

Citrus Sesame Salmon with Pak Choi

1 tsp coconut oil
4 salmon fillets
2 garlic cloves, sliced
1 tbsp grated fresh
   root ginger
1 star anise
juice of 2 oranges
sea salt

Pak choi
1 tsp coconut oil
400g baby pak choi
3 garlic cloves, sliced
1 tbsp soy sauce
1 tbsp sesame seeds

1 Heat the coconut oil in a frying pan. Add the salmon fillets, skin-side down, and fry them for 4 minutes. Turn the fish over, add the garlic, ginger, star anise and orange juice to the pan and cook for a couple of minutes longer. Remove the fish from the pan. By this time the juices should be reduced and syrupy but if not, keep the pan over the heat for another minute or so. Season the juices with a touch of salt.

2 Heat a teaspoon of coconut oil in a clean pan and stir-fry the pak choi for 3–4 minutes. Add the garlic and cook for a further minute, then add the soy sauce.

3 Serve the salmon on top of the pak choi, drizzle over the juices and finally sprinkle over the sesame seeds.

The subtle spicing in this recipe doesn't overpower the oily salmon fillets and the beautiful marinade works well with any fish – it's good with chicken too. The spinach side dish is bulked out with chickpeas, making this an economical treat to serve up for the family and perfect for a quick and easy midweek supper. **SERVES 4**

Masala Spiced Fish with Coconut Spinach

4 salmon fillets

Marinade
1 tbsp garam masala
1 tsp ground coriander
1 tsp paprika
$1/2$ tsp turmeric
2 garlic cloves, crushed
1 tbsp grated fresh
   root ginger
150ml natural yoghurt

Coconut spinach
1 tsp coconut oil
1 onion, sliced
2 garlic cloves, crushed
1 x 400g can of chickpeas
1 tsp garam masala
large bag of baby
   spinach, washed
200ml coconut milk
sea salt
black pepper

1 Mix the spices for the marinade in a large bowl with the garlic, ginger and yoghurt. Add the salmon steaks and leave them to marinate for 20 minutes. Preheat the oven to 200°C/180°C Fan/Gas 6.

2 Remove the salmon fillets from the marinade, place them on a non-stick baking tray and roast in the preheated oven for 10–12 minutes.

3 Meanwhile, cook the spinach. Heat the oil in a large saucepan, add the onion and garlic and cook over a medium heat for 3–4 minutes. Add the chickpeas and garam masala and stir well, then pile the spinach into the pan and cook for 1–2 minutes until wilted. Pour in the coconut milk and cook until the liquid has reduced. Season with salt and pepper.

4 Serve the salmon with generous helpings of coconut spinach.

This is a quick and tasty dish that the whole family will love. These courgette 'noodles' are a tasty low-carb alternative to spaghetti and can be used in any pasta recipe. They're fantastic with the herby olive-crusted cod or you can toss them with some pesto or a spicy tomato sauce. There are two quick and easy ways of cutting vegetables such as courgettes into slender ribbons – by using a simple julienne peeler or a vegetable spiralizer. Both are available online so check them out. SERVES 4

Herb-crusted Fish with Courgette 'Noodles'

80g light cream cheese
2 tbsp chopped fresh parsley
grated zest of $1/2$ lemon
80g green olives, pitted
    and chopped
4 fillets of white fish, such as
    cod or haddock, skinned
40g wholemeal
    breadcrumbs
3 courgettes
1 tbsp coconut oil
1 garlic clove, crushed
100g cherry tomatoes
squeeze of lemon juice
1 tbsp olive oil, for dressing
    (optional)
fresh basil, to garnish
sea salt
black pepper

1 Preheat the oven to 200°C/180° Fan/Gas 6. Put the cream cheese in a small bowl, then add the parsley, lemon zest and olives and mix well. Place the fish fillets on a baking tray, spread them with the cream cheese mixture, then sprinkle the breadcrumbs on top. Put the fish in the oven and bake for 12–14 minutes or until cooked through.

2 Meanwhile, use a julienne peeler or vegetable spiralizer to cut the courgettes into ribbons to make your 'noodles'. Place a large saucepan over a medium heat, add the coconut oil and cook the courgettes for 3–4 minutes. Add the garlic and tomatoes, cook for another minute or so, then season with salt, pepper and a small squeeze of lemon juice.

3 To serve, place a portion of courgette 'noodles' in each bowl and top with a piece of fish. Drizzle over some olive oil if you like and garnish with fresh basil.

It may sound strange, but the smoky flavour of chorizo goes brilliantly with shellfish and the combo makes this simple dish a real winner. Pasta always makes for a quick and easy supper, and if you like you can tweak this recipe to include your own favourite ingredients, such as chicken instead of prawns. You can also add extra seasonal vegetables. **SERVES 4**

Creamy Prawn and Chorizo Linguine

280g wholewheat linguine
1 tsp coconut oil
1 red onion, diced
5 garlic cloves, crushed
400g raw, shelled prawns
100g chorizo, cut into cubes
100ml white wine (optional)
2 tbsp low-fat mascarpone
  cheese
100g sunblush tomatoes
fresh basil, to garnish
  (optional)
sea salt
black pepper

1 Cook the pasta in lots of boiling, salted water according to the packet instructions. Drain, reserving some of the cooking water in case you need to loosen the sauce a little.

2 While the pasta is cooking, heat the coconut oil in a saucepan and gently fry the onion for 3–4 minutes until softened but not coloured. Add the garlic, prawns and chorizo and cook for another 3 minutes.

3 Pour in the white wine and continue to cook until the liquid is reduced by three quarters – if you don't want to include wine, use a little of the cooking water instead. Add the mascarpone cheese and tomatoes, season with salt and pepper, then stir until combined.

4 Add the drained pasta to the pan and toss it well to coat it with the sauce. Serve with some fresh basil if you like.

It's a waste of time to use white fish for this dish, as the spices tend to overpower its delicate flavour, but salmon can stand up to the fiery heat and spice of this curry from Goa. I love fish curries as they are so quick and easy to make. This really is a curry in a hurry! **SERVES 4**

Goan Fish Curry

1 tbsp coconut oil
1 onion, diced
3 garlic cloves, crushed
1 tbsp grated fresh
    root ginger
1 red chilli, deseeded and
    finely diced (optional)
2 tbsp garam masala
1/2 tsp turmeric
1 green pepper, deseeded
    and cut into 8 pieces
1 x 500g carton of
    tomato passata
200ml vegetable stock
1 tbsp tamarind paste
50g shredded coconut
200g salmon fillet, skinned
    and cut into 2.5cm cubes
200g raw, shelled prawns
2 large ripe tomatoes,
    quartered
fresh coriander, to garnish

1 Heat the coconut oil in a frying pan and cook the onion for 2–3 minutes. Add the garlic, ginger and chilli, if using, and cook for a further minute. Add the garam masala, turmeric and green pepper and cook for a minute more.

2 Pour in the passata and stock, then add the tamarind and shredded coconut. Bring everything to a gentle simmer, cover the pan with a lid and cook for about 15 minutes.

3 Add the fish, prawns and tomatoes to the pan and cook for 4–5 minutes until the fish has cooked through. Serve garnished with some fresh coriander.

Stir-fry recipes really are fast food. The key to a great stir-fry is all in the preparation – get everything ready before you start cooking and cut all the ingredients to the same size so they cook evenly. Heat your wok or non-stick pan until sizzling and you'll have a meal that's ready in minutes and tastes much better than a takeaway. **SERVES 4**

Firecracker Pork Stir-fry

1 heaped tsp coconut oil
1 pork tenderloin (about 400g), thinly sliced
1 thumb-sized piece of fresh root ginger (about 25g), cut into matchsticks
2 garlic cloves, finely sliced
1 carrot, cut into matchsticks
3 spring onions, sliced
1 red chilli, sliced (optional)
1 green pepper, sliced into thin strips
1 red pepper, sliced into thin strips
2 tbsp soy sauce
juice of $1/2$ lime
4 portions of egg noodles
1 tbsp toasted sesame seeds
fresh coriander, to garnish (optional)
lime wedges, to serve
sea salt
black pepper

1 Heat the coconut oil in a large pan and fry the slices of pork for 3–4 minutes until golden and cooked through. Add the ginger, garlic, carrot, spring onions, chilli, if using, and the peppers and cook for a minute or 2 before adding the soy sauce. Stir to combine, then add the lime juice. Season with salt and black pepper to taste.

2 Meanwhile, cook the noodles according to the packet instructions, then drain well.

3 Serve the stir-fried pork and vegetables on top of the egg noodles and sprinkle with sesame seeds. Serve garnished with fresh coriander, if using, and lime wedges

Meatballs are comfort food at the best of times but when smothered in this sticky hoisin glaze they are taken to another level. Any sort of mushrooms can be used to bulk this out so if you can't find oyster, try chestnut, shiitake or even good old button mushrooms are fine.

SERVES 4

Hoisin-glazed Meatballs with Noodles

400g turkey mince
1 egg yolk
2 tbsp chopped fresh coriander, plus extra to garnish
1 tsp Chinese 5-spice powder
1 tbsp grated fresh root ginger
2 garlic cloves, crushed
1–2 tsp coconut oil
150g oyster mushrooms, wiped and sliced
2–3 tbsp hoisin sauce
soy sauce, to taste
juice of 1/2 lime
4 nests of egg noodles
4–5 spring onions, finely sliced
sea salt
black pepper

1 Put the mince in a bowl, add the egg yolk, chopped coriander, 5-spice, ginger and garlic and mix well. Season with salt and pepper. Shape the mixture into golf ball-sized meatballs, then leave them to chill in the fridge for 20 minutes to help set the shape.

2 Heat the coconut oil in a frying pan and fry the meatballs over a medium heat for about 10 minutes. Add the mushrooms and cook for a further 5 minutes, turning occasionally until the meatballs are golden all over and cooked through. Pour in the hoisin sauce, soy, and lime juice, then toss to make sure everything is fully combined.

3 Cook the noodles according to the packet instructions, then drain well. Serve them into bowls, add the meatballs and garnish with spring onions and some more coriander.

Pho is a Vietnamese noodle soup. A good pho relies on a fantastic stock as a base, so try to make your own or invest in a good-quality shop-bought version. Be careful with stock cubes as they can be very salty – at least if you make your own stock you know exactly what has gone into it. I like to make a big pot of pho and freeze it in portions. This amazing dish also works well with prawns. **SERVES 4**

Vietnamese Beef Pho

1 tsp coconut oil
1 tbsp grated fresh
    root ginger
1 red chilli deseeded
    and sliced (optional),
    plus extra to serve
4 garlic cloves, crushed
1 onion, finely diced
1 lemon grass stalk
1 star anise
1 cinnamon stick
1 litre of good-quality
    beef stock
160g dried rice noodles
250g beef fillet, very
    thinly sliced
1–2 limes
1 tbsp soy sauce
100g beansprouts
fresh mint leaves, to serve
6 spring onions, finely sliced

1 Heat the oil in a large saucepan and the ginger, chilli, if using, the garlic and onion. Bash the lemon grass and add it to the pan along with the star anise and cinnamon and fry for 3–4 minutes over a medium heat. Add the stock to the pan and bring it to the boil, then reduce the heat to a simmer and cook for 20 minutes to allow the flavours to infuse.

2 Soak the noodles in a bowl of just-boiled water for 5 minutes until tender, then drain and set aside.

3 Add the sliced beef to the saucepan and cook for about 3 minutes, then add lime juice and soy sauce to taste.

4 Divide the noodles between 4 bowls, then ladle the beefy broth on top. Garnish with beansprouts, fresh mint and sliced spring onions, then add more chilli if you like your pho scorching hot!

CHAPTER 4
DINNERS

Dinner, or tea as I grew up calling it, is often the one meal when all the family have a chance to sit round the table and enjoy some food together while chatting about the trials of the day. For many of us, dinner may be the biggest meal of the day, but in fact it's best not to have a huge mound of food in the evening. Smaller amounts should be fine if you've eaten well earlier in the day. As a rule of thumb, aim for a palm-sized portion of protein, a fist-sized portion of carbohydrate and about the same of vegetables. It's also important just to eat until you are satisfied, not until you are full!

After a long day at work, the last thing most of us want is lots of faffing about in the kitchen. Simple, quick, affordable meals are what's needed – especially if you have hungry young ones impatient for their food. Many of these dishes can be made with ingredients you can keep in your store cupboard, so there should be no need to give in to the temptation of a ready meal. I do suggest marinating ingredients in some of the recipes, but this is usually optional. However, even just a brief marinade can make a huge difference to a dish so try to include this if you can. And if you plan ahead, you can always stick your meat in the marinade before you leave for work in the morning so it can be absorbing those delicious flavours all day.

Picture this – the winter nights are closing in, you've had a long day at work, the kids are making a racket in the front room demanding their dinner. Does this sound familiar – or is that just my house? This hearty broth really hits the spot and is a perfect way to bring some cheer to the cold winter months. I often cook a massive pot of this so there's some left for lunch the next day. Just make sure you cut the vegetables to the same size, as this will help them cook evenly. The recipe below is vegetarian, but you can add some spicy chorizo if you fancy it. **SERVES 4**

Vegetable-packed Pearl Barley Broth

1 tsp coconut oil
2 onions, diced
2 large carrots, diced
3 celery sticks, diced
3 garlic cloves, crushed
1 tbsp fresh rosemary,
    chopped
1 tsp smoked paprika
200g pearl barley
1 x 500g carton of
    tomato passata
1 tbsp tomato purée
1 litre vegetable stock
200g kale or winter
    greens, shredded
chopped fresh parsley,
    to garnish
sea salt
black pepper

1 Warm the oil in a large saucepan, then add the onions, carrots, celery and garlic. Cook them gently over a low to medium heat for 5 minutes, then add the rosemary and paprika.

2 Stir in the pearl barley, add the passata, tomato purée and stock, then season with salt and pepper. Simmer gently for about 50 minutes or until the vegetables and pearl barley are cooked through.

3 Stir in the kale or winter greens and leave the broth to stand for a few minutes. Ladle the broth into bowls and serve garnished with fresh parsley.

I find harissa paste is a lifesaver when it comes to knocking up a quick, easy meal. I always have some on hand to flavour sweet and spicy tagines and salad dressings or even to spike through a mayonnaise to top a barbecued lamb burger. Made from chillies, garlic and various spices, including cumin, coriander and fennel, harissa is a store-cupboard standby worth having. If you find it a little too spicy for your taste, use a teaspoon of ground cumin instead. **SERVES 4**

North African Sweet Potato and Carrot Salad

2 sweet potatoes,
   cut into wedges
400g baby carrots,
   halved lengthways
1 tbsp olive oil
1 heaped tsp harissa paste
1/2 tsp ground cumin
   (or 1 tsp if not
   using harissa)
4 large handfuls of
   baby spinach
1 red onion, sliced (optional)
seeds from a pomegranate
100g feta cheese, crumbled
small bunch of fresh
   coriander, to garnish

Dressing
1 tbsp olive oil
juice of 1/2 lemon
sea salt
black pepper

1 Preheat the oven to 190°C/170°C Fan/Gas 5. Put the sweet potatoes in a bowl with the carrots, drizzle them with the olive oil, then spoon in the harissa paste and cumin. Stir to make sure everything is well covered, then bake in the oven for 45–50 minutes.

2 To make the dressing, whisk the oil and lemon juice in a small bowl and season with salt and pepper.

3 When you're ready to serve, pile the spinach in a bowl with the onion, if using, and toss with the dressing. Serve the spinach on to plates and top with the sweet potatoes and carrots. Scatter over the pomegranate seeds and feta cheese, then garnish with fresh coriander.

DEAN'S TIP
Here's how I remove the seeds from a pomegranate. Cut the pomegranate in half round its middle, hold a half at a time in a bowl of water and break out the seeds. This way you don't get covered in juice!

Slow-roasting tomatoes really intensifies their naturally sweet flavour. Combine them with a little cheese and a few store-cupboard ingredients and you can create this show-stopping centrepiece. Just add a simple green salad and enjoy. **SERVES 4**

Slow-roasted Tomato Filo Tart

12 plum tomatoes, halved
2 garlic cloves, crushed
2 tbsp fresh thyme, leaves
    picked from the stems
1 tbsp olive oil
20g melted unsalted butter
5 free-range eggs
4 sheets of filo pastry
5 spring onions, finely sliced
80g feta cheese, crumbled
100ml milk
fresh basil, to serve
    (optional)
sea salt
black pepper

1 Preheat the oven to 170°C/150°C Fan/Gas 3 ½. Put the tomato halves on a baking tray, scatter over the garlic and thyme and drizzle them with the olive oil. Season with salt and pepper, then roast for 40 minutes. Turn the oven up to 190°C/170°C Fan/Gas 5.

2 Grease a medium-sized ovenproof frying pan or a round baking dish with melted butter. Beat 1 of the eggs in a small bowl. Lay a sheet of filo in the pan or dish and brush it lightly with melted butter. Repeat until all the filo has been used up, overlapping each sheet so every side of the pan or dish has some filo hanging over it. Brush the top with some beaten egg.

3 Add the roasted tomatoes and the spring onions to the pan or dish, making an even layer over the filo, then crumble the cheese on top. Beat the remaining 4 eggs with the milk, season with salt and pepper and pour them on to the tart. Turn the edges of the filo over to cover the filling and brush with beaten egg.

4 Bake the tart in the oven for 30–35 minutes, then leave to cool slightly before cutting into slices. Garnish with fresh basil if you like before serving.

Cooking en papillote (French for 'in parchment') is a perfect way of preparing fish. Wrapping the fish in baking parchment with herbs and soy locks in flavour and makes it beautifully succulent. Although it's not traditional, I seal my fish first in a hot pan to improve the colour and texture. I like to do this, as I eat with my eyes first, but you don't have to. Ketjap manis is an Indonesian soy sauce and is slightly sweeter than the usual sort. You can buy it in supermarkets now so give it a go. It's good in stir-fries too. **SERVES 4**

Asian-baked Salmon Parcels

4 baby pak choi, halved
4 salmon fillets, skin removed
4 thin slices of fresh
    root ginger
4 spring onions, finely sliced
1/2 red chilli, sliced (optional)
2 tbsp olive oil
3 tbsp ketjap manis or
    soy sauce
fresh coriander, to garnish
    (optional)
1 lime, quartered, to serve

Sesame broccoli
1 tsp coconut oil
400g broccoli, separated
    into florets
3 garlic cloves, sliced
2 tbsp ketjap manis or
    soy sauce
1 tbsp toasted sesame seeds

1 Preheat the oven to 200°C/180°C Fan/Gas 6. Cut out 4 circles of baking parchment, each about 40cm in diameter.

2 Place a large baking sheet on your work surface and put 1 parchment circle on top. Add a couple pieces of pak choi on half of the circle, then top with a salmon fillet, a slice of ginger, some spring onions and a few slices of chilli, if using. Drizzle with some oil and ketjap manis or soy sauce, then add a splash of water. Fold the other half of parchment over the filling and crimp the edges tightly to seal. You can staple the edges if you find it easier. Repeat to make the remaining parcels, then bake them in the oven for 12–14 minutes.

3 When the parcels are nearly done, cook the broccoli. Heat a teaspoon of coconut oil in a saucepan, add the broccoli and cook for 1–2 minutes. Add 2 tablespoons of water and continue to cook until the water has evaporated. Add the sliced garlic and cook for another couple of minutes, then sprinkle with ketjap manis or soy sauce and sesame seeds.

4 Remove the parcels from the oven and tear them open, releasing all the lovely aromas. Sprinkle over the coriander, if using, and serve with the stir-fried broccoli and wedges of lime.

I like to cook delicate haddock fillets with a spicy tomato sauce. This is a beautiful light dish and a lovely way to serve fish. My family likes to eat a pile of spinach with the fish but any greens will go well. **SERVES 4**

Tomato and Olive Haddock

1 tsp coconut oil
1 onion, very finely diced
2 garlic cloves crushed
1 tbsp fresh rosemary,
    very finely chopped
1 x 400g can of chopped
    tomatoes
200ml vegetable stock
$1/2$ tsp chilli powder
    (optional)
4 haddock fillets
2 tbsp chopped fresh parsley
grated zest of $1/2$ lemon
100g pitted green and
    black olives
200g fresh baby spinach
sea salt
black pepper

1 Heat the oil in a frying pan – you need one with a lid for this recipe. Add the onion, garlic and rosemary to the pan and cook over a medium heat for 3–4 minutes. Reduce the heat, add the tomatoes, stock and chilli powder, then continue cooking for 8–10 minutes. Season with a touch of salt and pepper.

2 Season the haddock fillets and place them on top of the tomato sauce. Cover the pan with a lid and cook for about 8–10 minutes or until the fish is cooked through. Add the parsley, lemon zest and olives to the pan.

3 Put the spinach in a large pan with a splash of water and place on the heat until the the leaves have wilted. Drain and squeeze as much water out of the spinach as you can, then season. Serve the fish with the sauce and some spinach.

I think mackerel is so under used. It tastes good, it's high in omega-3 fatty acids, vitamins and other nutrients and it's cheap to buy. On hot summer evenings this is fantastic cooked on a barbecue, but as we can't rely on our British weather I've adapted the recipe for the oven. If all else fails, these flavours of the Caribbean will bring a little sunshine into our lives. The jerk marinade in this recipe also works well with other fish. SERVES 4

BBQ Jerk Mackerel

4 fresh mackerel,
   cleaned and gutted
bunch of fresh thyme
2 limes, sliced

Marinade
3 garlic cloves, crushed
1 tbsp grated fresh
   root ginger
1 tsp ground allspice
1 tbsp fresh thyme
1 red chilli, chopped
   (optional)
1/2 teaspoon ground
   nutmeg
1/2 tsp cinnamon
30ml olive oil
juice of 1 lime

Salsa
1 ripe mango
200g baby plum tomatoes
1 red onion
1 green chilli (optional)
handful of fresh coriander
30ml olive oil
juice of 1 lime
sea salt
black pepper

1 Using a sharp knife, score the mackerel flesh 4 or 5 times on each side, but don't cut right through the flesh. Stuff the cavity of each mackerel with sprigs of thyme and some of the slices of lime. Place the mackerel in a wide, shallow dish.

2 Mix the marinade ingredients together, pour them over the fish and leave to marinate for 20–30 minutes. Preheat the oven to 200°C/180°C Fan/Gas 6.

3 Put the remaining slices of lime in a baking tray, put the mackerel on top and bake for about 20 minutes or until cooked through. Towards the end of the cooking time, preheat the grill. Take the fish out of the oven and pop it under the hot grill for a couple of minutes to recreate the barbecue effect.

4 To make the salsa, finely chop the mango, tomatoes, onion, chilli, if using, and the coriander. Put them all in a large bowl, add the oil and lime juice, then season well with salt and pepper. Serve the mackerel with the salsa and perhaps a baked sweet potato.

Chermoula is a North African marinade/sauce that works beautifully with chicken and fish. It's made with loads of fresh herbs and spices, brought to life with a good squeeze of lemon juice, and I like to think of it as a version of pesto. Chickpeas are a great inexpensive store-cupboard ingredient and are useful for bulking out stews, salads or curries. Marinate the chicken first if you can to maximize the flavour, but if you don't have time this dish will still be delicious. **SERVES 4**

Chermoula Chicken Salad

4 chicken breasts, skinned
1 tsp coconut oil
1 x 400g can of chickpeas, drained and rinsed
1/2 red chilli, deseeded and chopped (optional)
1/2 red onion, sliced (optional)
2 tbsp low-fat plain yoghurt
2 handfuls of baby spinach, to serve
sea salt
black pepper

Chermoula sauce
3 tbsp chopped fresh coriander
3 tbsp chopped flat-leaf parsley
1/2 red onion, roughly chopped
3 garlic cloves
1 tsp smoked paprika
1/2 tsp cumin
1/2 tsp coriander
juice of 1/2 lemon
1 tbsp olive oil

1 Put all the chermoula ingredients in a blender or food processor and blitz to a paste.

2 Using a sharp knife, slash each chicken breast 4–5 times, but don't cut right through the flesh. Put the chicken breasts in a bowl, add half the chermoula sauce and leave them to marinate for about an hour if possible.

3 Preheat the oven to 200°C/180°C Fan/Gas 6. Heat an ovenproof frying pan with the coconut oil until piping hot, then add the chicken breasts top-side down and cook for 2–3 minutes until coloured. Turn the chicken over and put the pan in the oven for 12–14 minutes or until the breasts are cooked through. If you don't have an ovenproof pan, transfer the chicken to a baking tray after sealing.

4 Put the chickpeas in a saucepan and warm them through. Tip them into a large bowl and add the chilli, if using, the red onion and yoghurt. Stir in a couple of tablespoons of the reserved chermoula sauce and season with salt and pepper.

5 To serve, put a bed of baby spinach on each plate, top with some chickpeas, then chicken. Any leftover sauce can be served on the side.

Traditionally this tagine is sweetened with honey, but I'm using sweet potato and apricots to find the perfect balance of sweet and savoury for this classic North African dish. Served with couscous, it makes a real treat on a cold winter's night. The harissa paste is optional, as it can be quite fiery, but it does add a lovely depth of flavour to this recipe.   SERVES 4

Chicken and Sweet Potato Tagine

1 tsp coconut oil
1 large onion, finely chopped
4 garlic cloves, crushed
1 tbsp grated fresh
    root ginger
1 large sweet potato,
    cut into cubes
1 tsp smoked paprika
1 tsp ground cinnamon
1 tsp ground cumin
1 heaped tsp harissa
    paste (optional)
1 x 500g carton of tomato
    passata
1 x 400g tin of chickpeas
40g dried apricots, chopped
300ml chicken stock
4 chicken breasts, skinned
chopped fresh coriander,
    to garnish
sea salt
black pepper

Couscous
150g wholewheat couscous
300ml chicken stock
juice of 1 lemon
1 tbsp extra virgin olive oil

1 Heat the oil in a heavy-based pan and fry the onion, garlic, ginger and sweet potato until softened. Add the spices and harissa, if using, then cook for 1–2 minutes.

2 Add the tomato passata, chickpeas, apricots and stock and bring the stock to a simmer. Cut the chicken breasts into bite-sized pieces and add them to the pan. Cover the pan with a lid and cook for 1 hour over a low heat. Just before serving, season with salt and pepper and garnish with fresh coriander.

3 Put the couscous in a heatproof bowl. Bring the stock to the boil, then pour it over the couscous. Cover the bowl with cling film and leave the couscous to stand for 5 minutes to absorb the stock. Fork it through to separate the grains, then stir in the lemon juice and oil and season with salt and pepper. Serve with the chicken.

There are some terrible commercial pestos available these days and to my mind none of them come even remotely close to recreating the zing of a freshly made version. My twist comes with the addition of peppery rocket and walnuts. This makes a lot of pesto so you could cook up a little more pasta than specified and there's tomorrow's lunch sorted! SERVES 4

Sticky Lemon Chicken with Walnut Pesto

4 chicken breasts, skinned
juice and zest of 1 lemon
1 tbsp olive oil
1 tsp coconut oil
1 tbsp honey
240g wholewheat linguine
fresh basil, to serve
grated Parmesan cheese,
    to serve (optional)
sea salt
black pepper

Walnut pesto
large bunch of fresh basil
2 handfuls of fresh rocket
50g walnuts
1/2 garlic clove
lemon juice, to taste
50ml extra virgin olive oil
30g Parmesan cheese,
    grated

1 Put the chicken breasts in a bowl with the lemon juice, zest and oil and set aside while the flavours develop. An hour is ideal but if you're short of time, 20 minutes will do.

2 Preheat the oven to 200°C/180°C Fan/Gas 6. Heat the coconut oil in an ovenproof frying pan. Remove the chicken from the marinade and season, then place it top-side down in the hot pan. Cook the chicken breasts for about 3 minutes until golden, then turn them over and spread them with the honey. Put the pan in the oven and bake the chicken for 12–14 minutes or until cooked through. If you don't have an ovenproof pan, seal the chicken in a frying pan, then transfer it to a baking tray.

3 To make the pesto, put the basil and rocket in a blender or food processor and add the walnuts, garlic, lemon juice and oil. Blitz to a loose paste, then add the Parmesan cheese and season to taste with salt and pepper. Set aside.

4 While the chicken is cooking, bring a large pan of salted water to the boil and cook the pasta according to the packet instructions. Drain, add the pesto and stir well. Slice the chicken and serve it with the pasta, fresh basil leaves and extra Parmesan cheese if you like.

Make sure you try this twist on traditional roast chicken. Whenever I roast a chicken I wonder why I don't do it more often – it's so delicious. Jazzing up the chicken with harissa paste takes a simple roast to a new level, but if you don't like the spicy kick, leave out the harissa and mix some cumin through the marinade. Some harissa pastes can be a bit fiery so watch out!

SERVES 4

Harissa Chicken with Hasselback Sweet Potatoes

1 tbsp harissa paste
3 garlic cloves, crushed
1 tbsp grated fresh
   root ginger
1 tbsp olive oil
juice of 1 lemon
1 chicken 1.5–2kg
4 medium sweet potatoes
1 tbsp olive oil
2 garlic cloves, crushed
1 tsp ground cumin
fresh coriander, plus
   extra to garnish
sea salt
black pepper

1 Mix the harissa, garlic, ginger, oil and lemon juice in a small bowl, then set aside. Place the chicken on a roasting tray, slash the thighs with a sharp knife, but don't cut right through the flesh, then rub the chicken all over with the paste. Cover the chicken with foil and refrigerate for at least 2 hours but overnight if you can.

2 Peel the sweet potatoes. Slice each potato at $1/2$–cm intervals along its length but be careful to cut only two-thirds of the way through so the slices remain attached at the base. Mix the oil, garlic and cumin in a bowl and season with salt and pepper, then rub this oil into the potatoes, making sure you coat them well. Set the potatoes aside.

3 Preheat the oven to 190°C/170°C Fan/Gas 5. Put the chicken in a roasting dish and stuff some fresh coriander and the squeezed lemon halves inside the cavity. Roast in the preheated oven for 45 minutes per kilogram, plus 20 minutes.

4 When the chicken has an hour left to cook, add the potatoes to the roasting dish and return it to the oven. After 30 minutes, run a fork across the top of the potatoes to fan them out – baste the chicken at the same time.

5 To check if the chicken is ready insert a skewer into the thickest part – the juices should run clear. If they're pink, pop the chicken back in the oven for 5 minutes and check again. Serve garnished with some fresh coriander.

This beautiful stew is a winner all year round. It's light and summery, but still hearty enough to warm your cockles on those dark autumn evenings. I love the smoky chorizo, which releases its paprika-rich oil and adds bags of flavour. If you want to cut the fat content, though, leave out the chorizo and add a little more smoked paprika. **SERVES 4**

Spanish Chicken Stew

1 tsp coconut oil
2 onions, sliced
5 garlic cloves, crushed
60g chorizo, sliced (optional)
5 fresh thyme sprigs
1 tsp smoked paprika
1 x 500g carton of
    tomato passata
1 tbsp tomato purée
500ml chicken stock
500g boneless chicken
    thighs or breasts, skinned
70g green olives, pitted
1 red pepper, deseeded
    and cut into large cubes
1 green pepper, deseeded
    and cut into large cubes
100g fennel, thinly sliced
sea salt
black pepper

1 Heat the oil in a large pan and fry the onions for 5 minutes. Add the garlic and chorizo and cook for another few minutes.

2 Stir in the thyme and paprika, then add the passata, tomato purée and stock. Bring everything to a simmer, then add the chicken, cover the pan and cook over a very low heat for 1 hour.

3 Add the olives, peppers and fennel to the pan and cook for another 10 minutes. Season with salt and pepper to taste before serving. This is lovely with cauliflower rice (see p. 110).

If you need a reminder of beautiful sunny holidays in the Med, try this recipe which brings a touch of sunshine to even the bleakest of British summer days. The dressing adds a welcome touch of acidity to the naturally sweet vegetables. This is a firm favourite for a Sunday lunch in our house, as it makes a change from a roast and it's all cooked in one tray so there's not much washing up! SERVES 4

Mediterranean Chicken Tray Bake

100g low-fat cream cheese
1 tbsp chopped parsley
100g green olives, pitted
   and chopped
4 chicken breasts, skinned
60g wholewheat
   breadcrumbs
400g new potatoes
1 red pepper, deseeded
   and cut into quarters
1 green pepper, deseeded
   and cut into quarters
2 red onions, quartered
1 tbsp olive oil
150g cherry tomatoes
   on the vine
1 bulb of garlic, cut in half
sea salt
black pepper

Dressing
2 tbsp olive oil
1 tbsp sherry vinegar
1 tsp honey
1 tsp wholegrain mustard
1/2 tsp smoked paprika

1 Put the cream cheese in a bowl with the parsley and olives and mix well. Spread the mixture over the chicken breasts, then sprinkle the breadcrumbs on top. Place the chicken breasts on a large baking tray.

2 Preheat the oven to 190°C/170°C Fan/Gas 5. Bring a large pan of salted water to the boil, add the potatoes and boil them for 8–10 minutes. Drain, then cut the potatoes in half lengthways and put them in a bowl with the peppers and onions. Drizzle them with the oil and season, then toss so they are all thoroughly coated with oil.

3 Scatter the veg into the baking tray with the chicken add the tomatoes and garlic, then roast for 45–50 minutes or until the chicken is cooked through.

4 Whisk the dressing ingredients in a small bowl and stir the dressing into the roasted veg before serving with the chicken.

Spaghetti bolognese has been a favourite in Britain for many years and I for one grew up eating this dish. I know the version we're used to eating is far removed from the Italian classic but I'm not about to make any apologies for my recipe with economical turkey mince. It tastes fantastic! **SERVES 4**

Lean Turkey Bolognese

1 tsp coconut oil
1 large onion, finely diced
2 large carrots, cut into small dice
3 celery sticks, cut into small dice
500g lean turkey mince
5 garlic cloves, crushed
1 x 500g carton of tomato passata
300ml beef stock
2 heaped tbsp tomato purée
100g mushrooms, sliced
1 tbsp dried oregano
1 tbsp chopped fresh rosemary
240g wholemeal spaghetti
small handful of fresh basil leaves, torn (optional but delicious)
sea salt
black pepper

1 Heat the oil in a large saucepan and cook the onion, carrots and celery for 5–6 minutes over a medium heat. Add the turkey mince and garlic, then cook for a couple more minutes.

2 Pour in the tomato passata and stock, then add the tomato purée, mushrooms, oregano and rosemary. Stir to combine. Bring everything to a simmer, then cover the pan and cook over a low heat for 1 hour. Season with salt and pepper.

3 Cook the pasta in boiling, salted water according to the packet instructions. Drain, then toss with the sauce. Serve at once with some freshly torn basil if you like.

Chilli con carne is another dish that has become a family favourite in recent years. My recipe, with lean turkey mince, is a good way to cut down the fat content of the traditional beef version and it's easy on the wallet too. Cauliflower 'rice' is a perfect low-carb alternative to rice and takes just minutes to make. I like to serve mine with some sliced fresh chilli and a dollop of yoghurt. **SERVES 4**

Banging Turkey Chilli with Cauliflower 'Rice'

1 tsp coconut oil
500g turkey mince
1 large onion, diced
4 garlic cloves, crushed
1 green pepper, deseeded
 and finely diced
1 tsp smoked paprika
1 tsp ground cumin
1 tsp ground cinnamon
1–2 tsp chilli powder
 (optional)
1 tsp dried oregano
1 x 500g carton of
 tomato passata
2 tbsp tomato purée
400g can of red kidney
 beans, drained and rinsed
300ml beef stock
2 tbsp chopped fresh
 coriander, to garnish
4 tbsp Greek yoghurt,
 to serve

Cauliflower 'rice'
1 small cauliflower grated

1 Heat the oil in a large pan and brown the turkey mince. Transfer it to a bowl, draining off any excess fat.

2 In the same pan, fry the onion, garlic and pepper for 3–4 minutes, then add the paprika, cumin, cinnamon, chilli powder and oregano and cook for another minute. Put the mince back in the pan and add the passata, tomato purée, kidney beans and stock. Cover and cook over a low to medium heat for at least an hour – the longer the better.

3 To prepare the cauliflower, grate it into a bowl that can go in the microwave, add 30ml of water and cover tightly with cling film. Microwave for 3–4 minutes. If you don't have a microwave, cook the grated cauliflower for 4–5 minutes in a dry pan over a medium heat, stirring often.

4 Garnish the chilli with fresh coriander and serve with dollops of Greek yoghurt and the cauliflower 'rice'.

Yes, I'm messing about with a classic cottage pie but don't worry –
this is great and packed full of Caribbean sunshine. The sweet potato
topping is rich in fibre and vitamins A and C, so is a healthy alternative
to a standard white potato. Its sweetness works well with the amazing
jerk spices to make this pie a winter crowd pleaser. SERVES 4

Caribbean Cottage Pie

1–2 tsp coconut oil
500g lean beef mince
1 large onion, diced
1 green pepper, deseeded
    and cut into small dice
1 red pepper, deseeded
    and cut into small dice
4 garlic cloves, crushed
1 tbsp grated fresh
    root ginger
1 tbsp fresh thyme leaves
1 tbsp red wine vinegar
1 tbsp jerk paste
400ml reduced-fat
    coconut milk
1 x 500ml carton of
    tomato passata
1 tsp ground allspice
sea salt
black pepper

Topping
500g sweet potatoes
$\frac{1}{2}$ tsp ground cinnamon
2 tbsp chopped fresh
    coriander, plus extra
    to garnish

1 Heat the oil in a large pan and brown the mince
for 5–6 minutes. Remove the mince from the pan
and set it aside.

2 Add the onion, peppers, garlic and ginger to the
pan with a little more oil if needed and cook for 5
minutes. Add the thyme, vinegar, jerk paste, coconut
milk, passata and allspice and bring everything to
a simmer. Put the mince back in the pan and cook
for 15–20 minutes until the mixture has thickened.
Season with salt and pepper.

3 Peel the sweet potatoes and cut them into even-
sized pieces. Put them in a pan of salted water, bring
them to the boil and cook for 12–15 minutes or until
tender. Drain, then leave the potatoes in a colander to
steam for 2–3 minutes. Mash them well or pass them
through a ricer, then stir in the cinnamon and coriander
and season with a pinch of salt and pepper.

4 Preheat the oven to 200°C/180°C Fan/Gas 6. Tip
the beef mixture into an ovenproof baking dish and
top with the sweet potato mash. Roughen up the
surface with a fork, then bake the pie for 30 minutes
or until the top is lovely and brown. Garnish with
a little more coriander when serving.

There's nothing more comforting than a luscious pie with a velvety filling. I use fresh herbs to bring flavour to my turkey pie, but you can substitute dried herbs if you prefer – just use half the amount. It doesn't matter much what kind of mushrooms you use. They all have different flavours so experiment and find out what you like best. You can also make a large pie instead of individual ones if you prefer. **SERVES 4**

Turkey and Mushroom Filo Pie

500g turkey breast, cut into cubes
1 heaped tbsp plain flour
1–2 tsp coconut oil
250g mixed mushrooms, such as chestnut, Portobello or shiitake, sliced
1 leek, shredded
2 garlic cloves, crushed
5 sprigs of fresh thyme
300ml chicken stock
1 tsp English mustard
2 tbsp chopped fresh tarragon
2 tbsp low-fat cream cheese
4 sheets of filo pastry
15g butter, melted
sea salt
black pepper

1 Put the cubes of turkey in a bowl. Season the flour, add it to the bowl and toss so that the turkey cubes are coated with flour. Heat the oil in a large pan and brown the turkey all over – do this in batches so you don't overcrowd the pan, setting each batch aside on a plate while you brown the rest.

2 Brown the mushrooms in the same pan, then add the leek, garlic and thyme and continue cooking for a few more minutes until the veg have softened.

3 Pour in the stock and bring it to a simmer, then put the turkey back in the pan and add the mustard and tarragon. Cook for 10–15 minutes, then stir in the cream cheese and season with salt and pepper. Preheat the oven to 190°C/170°C Fan/Gas 5.

4 Divide the turkey mixture into 4 individual ovenproof dishes, then top each one with a scrunched up sheet of filo. Brush the filo with melted butter. Bake the pies in the preheated oven for 20–25 minutes or until golden brown. These are lovely served with seasonal greens and roasted carrots.

When I was testing the recipes for my book this one really hit the spot with my family. I guarantee that if you try it once it will become a regular in your house too. It's one of my favourite things to eat – crunchy, colourful and a beautiful balance of hot, sweet, salty and sour flavours. Best of all, it's super-healthy, as by keeping most of the ingredients raw you are maximizing the nutritional value. I know it looks like a lot of ingredients but there's nothing difficult and there's very little cooking to do. I use a julienne peeler to prepare the carrot and mango. **SERVES 4**

Thai Beef and Mango Salad

1 garlic clove, crushed
2 tbsp soy sauce
juice of $\frac{1}{2}$ lime
200g sirloin steak, trimmed of fat
1 tsp coconut oil
100g vermicelli rice noodles
1 red pepper, deseeded and sliced into strips
1 green pepper, deseeded and sliced into strips
1 red onion, thinly sliced
1 large carrot, cut into thin strips (julienned)
100g beansprouts
100g sugarsnap peas, sliced lengthways
1 mango, peeled and cut into thin strips (julienned)
1 red chilli, deseeded and sliced (optional)
fresh coriander, to serve

Dressing
1 tbsp mango chutney
1 tbsp soy sauce
2 tbsp olive oil
1 garlic clove, crushed
juice of 1 lime

1 Mix the garlic, soy sauce and lime juice in a bowl and add the steak. Leave the steak to marinate for an hour if possible, but 20 minutes while you prepare the vegetables will do.

2 Heat a frying pan, add the coconut oil and cook the steak for 2–3 minutes on each side for medium – or a minute or so more or less for well-done or rare steak. Remove the steak from the pan and set it aside to rest for 5 minutes, then slice thinly.

3 Cook the noodles according to the packet instructions, then drain and leave to cool.

4 Whisk together the ingredients for the dressing. Pile the peppers, onion, carrot, beansprouts, sugarsnaps, mango and chilli, if using, in a bowl and toss with the dressing. Serve the salad with strips of beef and garnish with the coriander.

Argentinian beef is famous the world over and works beautifully with chimichurri sauce – they're a match made in heaven. The sauce is a little like salsa verde, but more punchy, with the tangy vinegar and a smoky hit of paprika. Serve with a lovely side salad. SERVES 4

Chimichurri Beef with Lime-griddled Corn

2 sirloin or rump steaks, trimmed of excess fat
olive oil
lime, cut into wedges, to serve

Chimichurri sauce
2 small shallots, peeled
3 garlic cloves, peeled
50ml red wine vinegar
small bunch of fresh coriander, plus extra to garnish
small bunch of flat-leaf parsley, plus extra to garnish
1/2 tsp paprika
30ml olive oil
sea salt
black pepper

Lime-griddled corn
4 corn cobs
1 tbsp olive oil or butter
1 red chilli, deseeded (optional)
juice of 1 lime
2 garlic cloves, crushed

1 To make the sauce, blitz the shallots, garlic, vinegar, herbs and paprika in a blender or food processor. Add olive oil until the sauce reaches a loose consistency. Season with salt and pepper and set half of the sauce aside for serving.

2 Transfer the rest of the sauce to a zip-seal freezer bag, add the steaks and leave them to marinate in the fridge for 1 hour.

3 Boil the corn in a large pan of salted water for about 5 minutes, then drain. Mix the olive oil or butter, chilli, if using, lime juice and garlic in a small bowl. Preheat a griddle pan until screaming hot, then brush the corn cobs with some of the oil or butter mixture and cook them for 8–10 minutes, turning them occasionally and basting them with more mixture. Season with salt and black pepper.

4 Take the steaks out of the bag, discarding any excess marinade. Heat a frying pan until very hot, add a dash of olive oil, then cook the steaks for 3–4 minutes on each side or to your liking. Remove the steaks from the pan, cover them with foil and leave them to rest for 5 minutes.

5 Slice the steaks and drizzle them with the rest of chimichurri sauce. Serve with the corn and garnish with some lime wedges and herbs.

The next few recipes are all delicious side dishes that can be served with the main meal ideas in this chapter. This scrumptious slaw looks every bit as good as it tastes. **SERVES 4**

Broccoli, Apple and Walnut Slaw

1 small red onion,
  very finely sliced
1/2 red chilli, finely
  diced (optional)
1 small head of broccoli,
1 Granny Smith apple
50g walnuts, crushed slightly
100ml low-fat Greek yoghurt
1 tsp wholegrain mustard
squeeze of lemon juice,
  to taste
sea salt
black pepper

1 Put the onion and chilli, if using, in a large bowl. Grate the broccoli and apple and add them to the bowl with the walnuts, then mix everything together well.

2 Mix the yoghurt, mustard and lemon juice in a small bowl, then stir the mixture into the salad. Season with salt and pepper and serve.

We don't often think of cooking lettuce but these griddled baby gems taste amazing and the blue cheese dressing sets them off a treat. Dolcelatte is an Italian blue cheese and is available in most supermarkets. Buttermilk, too, is available in supermarkets. **SERVES 4**

Griddled Baby Gems with Blue Cheese

8 baby gem lettuces,
  halved lengthways
1 tbsp olive oil
sea salt
black pepper

Dressing
150ml buttermilk
2 tbsp mayonnaise
juice of 1/2 lemon
100g Dolcelatte cheese,
  crumbled
1/2 garlic clove, crushed
1 tbsp olive oil

1 Whisk the dressing ingredients together in a small bowl, then season with salt and pepper.

2 Preheat a griddle pan on the hob or a barbecue. Put the baby gems into a bowl, coat them with olive oil and season with salt and pepper. Place them on the griddle pan or barbecue and cook for about 5 minutes, turning them once.

3 Transfer the griddled lettuces to a serving plate then drizzle them with the blue cheese dressing.

As you can probably tell, I'm a big fan of sweet potatoes. This is one of my favourite ways of cooking them and it goes beautifully with anything from plain grilled chicken to sausages or fish. **SERVES 4**

Lemon and Cumin Roasted Sweet Potatoes

2 large sweet potatoes
2 tbsp olive oil
1 tsp harissa paste
1 tsp ground cumin
grated zest and juice
  of $1/2$ lemon
sea salt
black pepper

1 Peel the sweet potatoes and cut them into 2.5cm cubes. Put them in a bowl and add the oil, harissa and cumin. Season with salt and pepper and mix well until all of the potato cubes are coated with the spicy oil. Preheat the oven to 200°C/180°C Fan/Gas 6.

2 Line a baking tray with foil – cleaning the tray after roasting sweet potatoes can be nightmare! Tip the potatoes on to the tray and roast them for 40–45 minutes. Remove them from the oven and sprinkle with the lemon zest and juice before serving.

Green beans go well with almost anything and this is a great way of serving them. The lemon juice and toasted almonds add flavour and texture, making this a dish to savour. **SERVES 4**

Citrus Green Beans with Almonds

20g toasted flaked almonds
1 tsp coconut oil
300g green beans, trimmed
1 garlic clove, crushed
grated zest of 1/2 lemon
squeeze of lemon juice,
   to taste
sea salt
black pepper

1 Scatter the almonds in a dry frying pan and toast them briefly over a medium heat. Watch them carefully, as they burn easily. Remove and set aside.

2 Warm the coconut oil in a frying pan over a medium to high heat. Add the green beans and cook them for 1–2 minutes. Toss in the garlic and cook for a further minute, then pour in a small splash of water and continue cooking until the water has evaporated.

3 Add the lemon zest and a squeeze of juice to taste, then season with salt and pepper. Scatter over the toasted almonds.

CHAPTER 5
TAKEAWAY FAVOURITES

Whether we admit it or not, having someone cook for us is a pretty attractive prospect. But we have to take into account two things: the cost to our wallets and the cost to our health. I love a takeaway as much as anyone and we all like a night off from cooking for the family every now and then. When I was growing up, a takeaway was a massive treat in our household, and the smell of fish and chips soaked in lashings of vinegar and topped with copious amounts of tomato ketchup is one of my earliest and most cherished food memories. The problem is that some of us are now eating far more takeaways than that occasional treat back in the day.

Many of us opt for a trip to our local takeaway because we don't believe we can recreate the taste of our favourite dish at home. What are the ingredients that give the dishes that authentic takeaway flavour? Will we ever find out the secret blend of spices in the Colonel's fried chicken? There are a couple of reasons why takeaways taste the way they do – one being flavour enhancers such as MSG and another being the heavy-handed use of fats and sugars in the cooking. It is possible to make these fabulous dishes at home and though they might not be completely sin free they can be a damn sight healthier and cheaper than the takeaway versions. I believe that the satisfaction of making these recipes at home will add at least 10 per cent to the flavour.

Great pizza relies on quick cooking at extremely high oven temperatures. Unfortunately we can't recreate these temperatures at home so this trick of using a frying pan can help make that crisp base we associate with a takeaway pizza. Kids love to get involved too, so let them scatter on their own favourite toppings – but keep them well away from the hot pans! My daughter Indie loves to get creative with her toppings, often using peppers, cherry tomatoes and olives to create faces on hers, as well as making a big mess of the worktops along the way. MAKES 2 X 23CM PIZZAS

Mozzarella Deep-pan Pizzas

Base
250g strong wholemeal
   flour, plus extra for dusting
$1/2$ x 7g sachet of yeast
$1/2$ tsp salt
15ml olive oil
150ml warm water

Tomato sauce
1 tsp coconut oil
200g cherry tomatoes
$1/2$ red onion, diced
3 garlic cloves, crushed
1 tsp dried oregano
sea salt
black pepper

Topping
2 slices of Parma ham,
   torn into pieces
1 red onion, thinly sliced
1 mozzarella ball (150g),
   torn into pieces
fresh basil, to serve

1 Mix the flour, yeast and salt in a large bowl. Add the olive oil, then gradually add the water and mix to form a soft dough. Turn the dough out on to a lightly floured surface and knead for 5 minutes. Put the dough in a clean bowl and cover with a damp tea towel, then leave it to rise for about an hour.

2 To make the sauce, heat the oil in a pan over a low to medium heat and fry the tomatoes, onion and garlic for 3–4 minutes. Add the oregano and seasoning, then tip the sauce into a blender and blitz until smooth.

3 When the dough has risen, turn it out on to the work surface and knock out the air. Divide the mixture in half. Roll 1 piece out on a floured surface to a circle of about 23cm across, then repeat with the other ball of dough. Preheat the oven to 240°C/220°C Fan/Gas 9.

4 Heat a 25cm non-stick frying pan over a high heat and add 1 of the pizza bases. Cook for 1–2 minutes, then top with half the tomato sauce, making sure you leave a 1–2cm gap around the edge. Add some of the torn ham, onion and mozzarella. Repeat with the other pizza base and the rest of the toppings.

5 Cook the pizzas in the preheated oven for 5–6 minutes or until the crust is crisp and golden. Top with some fresh basil leaves before serving.

This simple curry is packed full of spinach and chickpeas which makes it both nutritious and economical. I often order it as a side dish when I push the boat out and have a curry at my local Indian but it's more than a vegetable accompaniment and makes a great meal in its own right. Serve with a portion of brown basmati rice and some yoghurt for a little hit of protein. **SERVES 4**

Chana Palak Curry

1 tbsp coconut oil
1 tsp ground cinnamon
1 tbsp garam masala
1 tsp cayenne pepper
1 tsp ground turmeric
2 onions, sliced
4 garlic cloves, chopped
2 tbsp grated fresh
　root ginger
2 x 400g cans of chickpeas,
　drained and rinsed
400g can of chopped
　tomatoes
1 tbsp tomato purée
200ml vegetable stock
1 bag of baby spinach
Greek yoghurt, to serve

1 Heat the coconut oil in a large pan over a medium heat, throw in the spices and cook them for a minute. Add the onions, garlic and ginger and continue cooking for 5 minutes.

2 Add the chickpeas, tomatoes, tomato purée and stock to the pan and bring everything to a simmer, then continue cooking for 10 minutes. Add the spinach to the pan and stir until the leaves have wilted. Serve with a dollop of Greek yoghurt.

This is one of the nation's favourite takeaways and probably the easiest to make at home. I remember eating the deep-fried version when I was growing up and yes, it might have been nice but this version tastes so much fresher and takes less time to put together than nipping down to the takeaway. The key to Chinese cooking is to get everything prepared then GO GO GO! Lightning-fast food. You can use shelled prawns or whole ones. If you use whole prawns, leave the heads and tails on but remove the dark veins down the back before cooking. **SERVES 4**

Sweet and Sour Prawns

1 tsp coconut oil
1 red pepper, deseeded
    and sliced
1 green pepper, deseeded
    and sliced
3 garlic cloves, crushed
1 tbsp grated fresh
    root ginger
500g raw tiger prawns
    (shelled weight)
30ml cider vinegar
30g soft brown sugar
4 tbsp tomato ketchup
200ml vegetable stock
1 tsp cornflour
100g beansprouts
5 spring onions, sliced,
    to garnish
sea salt
black pepper

1 Heat the oil in a frying pan, then fry the peppers for 1–2 minutes. Add the garlic, ginger and prawns and continue cooking for another 1–2 minutes or until the prawns have turned pink. Add the vinegar, sugar, ketchup and stock and give it all a good stir.

2 Dissolve the cornflour in 2 teaspoons of water, add the mixture to the pan and stir until the sauce has thickened. Add the beansprouts and cook for a further minute, then season with salt and pepper.

3 Garnish with the spring onions before serving with cauliflower rice (see p.110) or egg noodles.

Fish and chips were a big treat for my brother Wes and me when we were growing up. We'd run down to the chippie with great excitement, and on days when we didn't have much money a bag of 'scrumps' (Bristolians will know what I mean) did just as well. Scrumps are the leftover scrapings of fried batter and, looking back, not the healthiest of foods I realize. My version of fish and chips certainly cuts down on the unhealthy fats but is still a perfect Friday night treat. Loins are the thickest part of a white fish fillet and just right for this recipe.   SERVES 4

No-guilt Fish and Chips

50g plain flour
1 tsp smoked paprika
2 eggs, beaten
60g wholemeal
    breadcrumbs
50g Parmesan cheese,
    grated (optional)
4 firm white fish loins
    (preferably sustainable
    cod or haddock)
2–3 tbsp coconut oil
1 lemon, cut into wedges,
    to serve
sea salt
black pepper

Sweet potato chips
2–3 sweet potatoes
2 tbsp olive oil

Peas
100g smoked pancetta
300g frozen peas, defrosted
1 tbsp chopped fresh mint
2–3 spring onions,
    finely sliced
small squeeze of lemon juice

1 First the chips; preheat the oven to 200°C/180°C Fan/Gas 6. Peel the sweet potatoes and cut them into chip-sized chunks. Put them in a bowl, drizzle them with the oil and season with salt and pepper, then toss them thoroughly to make sure they're all well coated. Tip the chips on to a baking tray and cook them in the preheated oven for 30–40 minutes.

2 Now for the fish; put the flour in a bowl and season with salt, pepper and paprika. Put the beaten eggs in another bowl and place the breadcrumbs and grated Parmesan, if using, in a third bowl. When the chips are nearly ready, dip each piece of fish into the seasoned flour, then the beaten egg and finally the breadcrumbs. Heat a shallow layer of oil in a frying pan and cook the fish for 6–7 minutes, turning until golden on both sides. Drain on some kitchen paper.

3 While the fish is cooking, fry the pancetta in a small saucepan until crispy. Add the peas and heat them through, then add the mint, spring onions and lemon juice and season with salt and pepper.

4 I know it sounds lazy but we like to serve our fish and chips on a huge sheet of greaseproof paper with lashings of ketchup and some lemon wedges. When we're done we scrunch up the paper and shove it in the bin so no washing up – BONUS!!

For my low-carb version of prawn fried rice – a takeaway favourite – I use grated cauliflower instead of rice. You can add pretty much any meat or vegetables to this recipe so it's a good way of using up leftovers, such as shredded roast chicken from Sunday lunch. One of my favourite store-cupboard ingredients is sriracha, a type of hot chilli sauce. Supermarkets stock it now but if you can't find it in your local store, have a look in an Asian supermarket. It's great! **SERVES 4**

Toasted Cauliflower and Prawn Fried 'Rice'

1 large cauliflower, grated
2 tbsp coconut oil
400g shelled raw prawns
1/2 red onion, sliced
2 garlic cloves, crushed
100g frozen peas, defrosted
2 eggs, beaten
2 tbsp soy sauce
1 tbsp sriracha chilli sauce (optional)
3 spring onions, finely sliced
1 red chilli, deseeded and sliced (optional)
2 tbsp chopped coriander
sea salt
black pepper

1 Preheat the oven to 220°C/200°C Fan/Gas 7. Put the grated cauliflower in a large bowl. Melt 1 tablespoon of the coconut oil, add it to the cauliflower with some salt and pepper, then toss well so that all the cauliflower is coated with oil. Tip the cauliflower on to a baking tray and roast it in the preheated oven for 25–30 minutes.

2 Using a sharp knife, slit the back of each prawn and remove the black vein. Heat the rest of the coconut oil in a large non-stick pan. Add the prawns and cook them for 1–2 minutes until they start to turn pink. Add the onion, garlic and peas and cook for a couple of minutes, then add the toasted cauliflower and fry for 2 minutes more.

3 Move the cauliflower to one side and pour in the beaten eggs, stirring so the egg mixture breaks up and coats the rice. Add a dash of soy and sriracha sauce, if using, and sprinkle over the spring onions, chilli, if using, and the coriander.

This is my take on a warming Caribbean spiced chicken stew. I've loved jerk chicken ever since the smells wafting from the smoking barrels at the annual St Paul's Carnival in Bristol first made me fall in love with this cuisine. My brother Wesley cooks jerk chicken with a tomato-based sauce to help it go a little further, and the sauce mixed through the rice and peas is a revelation, believe me. Hope you enjoy it as much as I do. **SERVES 4**

Jerk Chicken Stew with Rice and Peas

1 tsp coconut oil
1 large onion, diced
3 garlic cloves, crushed
1 tbsp grated fresh
   root ginger
1 green pepper, diced
1 tbsp fresh thyme leaves
2 tbsp red wine vinegar
1 tbsp jerk paste
200ml reduced-fat
   coconut milk
1 x 500g carton of
   tomato passata
2 tbsp Worcestershire sauce
1 tsp ground allspice
4 chicken breasts, skin
   removed and meat cut
   into cubes, or 8 bone-in
   chicken thighs
2 sweet potatoes, diced
1–2 tbsp honey, to taste
sea salt
black pepper

Rice and peas
1 tsp coconut oil
1 onion, diced
240g brown basmati rice
small piece of fresh root
   ginger (about 15g),
   cut into 4–5 slices
3 sprigs of fresh thyme
200ml reduced-fat
   coconut milk
300ml vegetable stock
1 x 400g tin black eye
   beans drained

1 Heat the oil in a large pan, add the onion, garlic, ginger and pepper and cook for 5 minutes. Add the thyme, vinegar, jerk paste, coconut milk, passata, Worcestershire sauce and allspice, then bring to a simmer.

2 Add the chicken to the pan along with the sweet potatoes, cover the pan with a lid and cook over a very low heat for 1 1/2 hours. Remove the lid and cook for another 20 minutes to allow the sauce to thicken. Season and add honey to taste.

3 For the rice, heat the oil in a saucepan, add the onion and fry for 5 minutes until softened. Add the rice, ginger, thyme, coconut milk, stock and beans. Bring to a simmer, reduce the heat right down and cover the pan with a lid. Cook until all the liquid has evaporated and the rice is done – this will take about 30–35 minutes. Season with salt and pepper. Serve with the chicken stew.

Thai takeaways and restaurants are popping up all over the place in response to our love of street food and fragrant Thai-spiced dishes. You can get some fantastic curry pastes now in our high streets and supermarkets and they add amazing flavour to a speedy supper. And paired with some fresh ingredients, such as ginger, lemon grass and garlic, they can help homemade versions of these dishes can reach new heights. **SERVES 4**

Aromatic Chicken and Peanut Thai Curry

1 tbsp coconut oil
1 onion, diced
6 garlic cloves, crushed
1 red chilli, deseeded
   and diced (optional)
1 lemon grass stalk, bruised
1 tbsp grated fresh
   root ginger
400ml reduced-fat
   coconut milk
400ml chicken stock
1 tbsp soy sauce
2 tbsp red Thai curry paste
2 tbsp unsweetened
   peanut butter
2 chicken breasts, skinned
   and thinly sliced
150g fine green beans
1–2 limes
1 tbsp brown sugar, to taste
small bunch of fresh
   coriander, to serve
   (optional)

1 Heat a pan over a medium heat and add the coconut oil. Fry the onion, garlic, chilli, if using, lemon grass and ginger for about 5 minutes until softened. Pour in the coconut milk, stock, soy sauce, curry paste and peanut butter and bring to a gentle simmer.

2 Add the slices of chicken to the pan and cook for 10 minutes, then add the beans and continue to cook for a further 5 minutes. Add a good squeeze of lime juice and sugar to taste, to balance the flavours of the dish.

3 Stir in some fresh coriander, if using, then serve with wholegrain basmati rice.

Peri peri is a chilli marinade that has its roots in Portugal and is also popular in South Africa where my nan comes from. It was made very fashionable in the UK by a famous restaurant chain and this is a chance to recreate those flavours in your own home. You can make the marinade as hot or not as you like – leave out the chilli if you're not a fan, as the other spices will more than carry this recipe off. I like to pair the chicken with a creamy slaw, which balances out the heat. This dish also tastes amazing cooked on the barbecue if you get a chance. Lush! **SERVES 4**

Peri Peri Chicken with Red Cabbage Slaw

1 tsp coconut oil
4 chicken breasts, skinned

Peri peri marinade
2 red chillies (optional)
1 red pepper, deseeded
   and diced
1 tsp smoked paprika
4 garlic cloves, crushed
1 tbsp grated fresh
   root ginger
2 tbsp red wine vinegar
20ml olive oil
sea salt
black pepper

Red cabbage slaw
1/2 red cabbage, shredded
1 small red onion,
   very finely sliced
1 carrot, grated
1 apple, grated
2 tbsp finely chopped
   flat-leaf parsley
100ml 0% fat Greek yoghurt
1 tsp wholegrain mustard

1 Place all the peri peri marinade ingredients in a blender or food processor and blitz until you have a paste with a fine consistency. Put the chicken breasts in a bowl, pour in the marinade and leave in the fridge for at least 2 hours or better still overnight.

2 Preheat the oven to 200°C/180°C Fan/Gas 6. Heat the oil in an ovenproof pan on the hob and fry the breasts until nicely coloured. Turn them over and cook for a further minute, then put the pan in the preheated oven and cook the chicken for 12–14 minutes or until the breasts are cooked through.

3 While the chicken is cooking, put the cabbage, onion, carrot, apple and parsley in a bowl and mix well. Add the yoghurt and mustard and mix again to combine, then season with salt and pepper. Serve with the peri peri chicken.

The balti is a takeaway favourite and I'm sure you all know that the name balti comes from the dish this curry is served in. My version isn't loaded down with lots of ghee so isn't going to worry your waistline too much. Serve with brown basmati rice or my cauliflower 'rice' recipe (see p.110).

SERVES 4

Chicken Pepper Balti

1 tsp coconut oil
1 large onion, sliced
1 tsp ground cumin
1 tsp ground coriander
1 x 500g carton of
    tomato passata
200ml chicken stock
3 chicken breasts,
    skinned and sliced
3 fresh tomatoes, quartered
1 red pepper, deseeded
    and cut into 8
1 green pepper, deseeded
    and cut into 8
fresh coriander, to garnish

Curry paste
1 onion, roughly chopped
5 garlic cloves, peeled
1 thumb-sized piece
    of fresh root ginger
    (about 25g), peeled
1 red chilli (optional)
1 tsp cinnamon
1 tbsp garam masala
1 tsp fennel seeds
1 tsp turmeric
1 tsp coconut oil

1 Place all the curry paste ingredients in a blender or food processor and blitz to a fine paste. Set aside.

2 Heat the oil in a large pan and cook the onion for 5 minutes until softened, then add the curry paste, cumin and coriander and continue to cook over a medium heat for 3–4 minutes. Add the passata and stock and bring to a gentle simmer.

3 Add the slices of chicken, cover the pan and cook for 20 minutes. Remove the lid, add the fresh tomatoes and peppers, then cook for a further 10 minutes. Garnish with fresh coriander before serving.

This is my reduced-fat version of Britain's most popular curry – chicken tikka masala. OK, this is not totally guilt-free but a treat every now and then is fine in my book, and my recipe has far fewer calories than the curries from your local curry house. You can get some great curry pastes in supermarkets now so don't be afraid to use them. And if you have the time to marinate the chicken, the flavours will be incredible so it's worth planning ahead. SERVES 4

Chicken Tikka Masala

4 chicken breasts, skinned and diced
100g low-fat natural yoghurt
3 tbsp tikka masala paste (1 tbsp for marinade and 2 tbsp for sauce)
3 garlic cloves, crushed
juice of $1/2$ lemon
2 tsp coconut oil
2 onions, finely diced
3 garlic cloves, crushed
1 tbsp grated fresh root ginger
$1/2$ tsp ground turmeric
1 tsp ground cinnamon
1 x 500g carton of tomato passata
400ml reduced-fat coconut milk
40g ground almonds
pinch of sugar, to taste
fresh coriander, to garnish
sea salt
black pepper

1 Put the diced chicken in a bowl and mix with the yoghurt, a tablespoon of tikka masala paste, the garlic and lemon juice. Cover with cling film and leave the chicken to marinate in the fridge for at least 2 hours, but preferably overnight.

2 Heat a teaspoon of the coconut oil in a non-stick frying pan. Remove the chicken from the marinade and fry for 2–3 minutes on each side – you might need to do this in batches so you don't overcrowd the pan. Set the chicken aside.

3 Heat another teaspoon of coconut oil and fry the onions for 4–5 minutes, then add the garlic and ginger and cook for another 3–4 minutes. Add the turmeric, cinnamon and the remaining tikka paste and fry for another minute.

4 Pour in the passata, coconut milk and ground almonds, bring to a simmer, then add the chicken to the sauce. Cover the pan with a lid and simmer for 45 minutes. Add a pinch of sugar and some salt and pepper to taste, and then garnish with fresh coriander before serving.

These kebabs are nothing like the versions served on street corners up and down the country. They are healthy, fresh and taste much better for dinner than at two in the morning after a night on the tiles. The sauce is pungent but authentic, and of course you can leave out the chilli if you prefer. I was taught how to make these by a kind kebab shop owner a few years ago and I think they taste great – the hotter the better! Marinating is optional but the flavours really do develop if you have time to let the chicken sit in the spices. **SERVES 4**

Shawarma Chicken Kebabs

4 chicken breasts, each
   sliced into 5 pieces
4 flatbreads
1 small tub of hummus
1/2 cucumber, deseeded
   and diced, to serve
1 red onion, thinly sliced
   (optional), to serve
3 ripe plum tomatoes,
   deseeded and diced,
   to serve

Marinade
80ml low-fat plain yoghurt
2 garlic cloves, crushed
juice and zest of 1/2 lemon
1/2 tsp cumin
1/2 tsp dried oregano
1/2 tsp ground cinnamon

Chilli sauce
4 garlic cloves, crushed
1 small red onion, diced
2 red chillies, roughly
   chopped (optional)
1 fresh tomato, diced
1 red pepper, deseeded
   and roughly chopped
1 tsp dried chilli flakes
2 tbsp tomato purée
1 tbsp white wine vinegar
sea salt

1 Mix the marinade ingredients in a large bowl, add the slices of chicken and leave them in the fridge for a couple of hours. If you're going to use wooden skewers, leave them to soak in water.

2 Remove the chicken pieces and thread them on to the skewers. Preheat a griddle pan or a barbecue and cook the kebabs for 7–8 minutes on each side or until cooked through.

3 Put the sauce ingredients, except the salt, in a blender or food processor and blitz to a fine paste. Transfer the sauce to a small saucepan and heat it through for 3–4 minutes, adding water to loosen it if necessary. Season with a touch of salt to taste.

4 Toast the flatbreads and spread them with a dollop of hummus. Serve with the kebabs, some cucumber, slices of onion, if using, tomato and as much chilli sauce as you can handle!

Fried chicken has become very fashionable over the last few years, with loads of trendy street food vendors popping up and trying to recreate this classic from the American South. In my healthier version the chicken is baked until golden and crispy instead of being deep-fried. Buttermilk is available in supermarkets and helps to flavour and tenderize the meat. It really does make a difference so make sure you leave time to marinate the chicken so the buttermilk can work its magic. **SERVES 4**

Buttermilk Oven-fried Chicken

4 chicken breasts, skinned
200ml buttermilk
60g plain flour
30g Panko breadcrumbs
1/2 tsp salt
1/2 tsp black pepper
1/2 tsp cayenne pepper
1/2 tsp smoked paprika
1/2 tsp garlic powder
1 tsp onion powder
1 tsp dried thyme
2 tbsp coconut oil

1 Cut the chicken breasts in half, put them in a bowl and pour in the buttermilk. Leave them to marinate in the fridge for at least 2 hours but overnight if possible.

2 Preheat the oven to 200°C/180°C Fan/Gas 6. Mix all the dry ingredients in a bowl. Remove the chicken breasts from the buttermilk, shaking off most of the liquid, then toss them in the flour mixture.

3 Heat the coconut oil in a large non-stick pan, shake the excess flour off the chicken pieces and cook them for 2–3 minutes until they are beginning to turn golden. Turn the chicken pieces over and cook for a couple more minutes.

4 Remove the chicken from the pan and place it on a wire rack set over a baking tray. Bake in the preheated oven for 25–30 minutes or until cooked through. Sweet potato chips (see p.130) and some red cabbage slaw (see p.136) make great accompaniments.

This dish is usually cooked in the intense heat of a tandoor oven, but unless you're ready to dig a large pit in your garden to house one you'll need to make do with your regular oven. My recipe gives you a beautifully fragrant, fuss-free result and I love to serve this with a spinach, coriander and onion salad. Marinating the chicken will help develop the flavours but is not essential. **SERVES 4**

Tandoori Roast Chicken with Coconut Sambal

4 chicken breasts, skinned

Tandoori marinade
1 tbsp garam masala
1 tsp ground coriander
1 tsp chilli powder
1 tsp paprika
$\frac{1}{2}$ tsp ground turmeric
$\frac{1}{2}$ tsp ground cinnamon
100ml 0% fat Greek yoghurt
1 tbsp grated fresh
    root ginger
3 garlic cloves, crushed
juice of $\frac{1}{2}$ lemon

Coconut sambal
100g fresh coconut, grated
1 green chilli, deseeded
    (optional)
$\frac{1}{2}$ garlic clove,
    roughly chopped
1 tsp olive oil
small handful of
    fresh coriander
juice of 1 lime
sea salt

1 Mix the marinade spices in a large bowl, then stir in the yoghurt, ginger, garlic and lemon juice. Using a sharp knife, slash the chicken pieces in a few places – this allows the marinade to penetrate – but don't cut right through the flesh. Put the chicken portions in a large zip-seal freezer bag and add the tandoori marinade. Massage the marinade into the chicken through the bag, then refrigerate for at least 2 hours or overnight if you can.

2 Preheat the oven to 190°C/170°C Fan/Gas 5. Place the chicken portions on a baking tray and bake in the preheated oven for 50–60 minutes or until cooked through. Take the chicken out of the oven and leave it to rest for 5 minutes before serving.

3 To make the sambal, put all the ingredients, except the salt, in a blender or food processor with about a tablespoon of water. Blitz until the mixture forms a paste but still retains some texture. Season with salt and leave to stand for at least 10 minutes before serving with the chicken and a nice green side salad.

Char sui is a Chinese barbecue dish with complex Asian flavours and I like to make it with pork tenderloin – a great cut of meat that goes a long way. I suggest using two fillets, but that's the glutton in me. One will still go a long way. I've been eating fried quinoa as a substitute for rice for ages and I think it tastes amazing. It's a brilliant source of protein too. SERVES 4

Char Sui Pork with Quinoa Fried 'Rice'

2 pork tenderloins
pak choi or other greens,
    to serve

Marinade
1 tbsp grated fresh
    root ginger
3 garlic cloves, crushed
1 tbsp hoisin sauce
50ml sherry
2 tbsp soy sauce
1 heaped tsp Chinese
    5-spice powder

Quinoa fried 'rice'
200g quinoa
1 tbsp coconut oil
100g frozen peas,
    defrosted
50g bean sprouts
2 eggs, beaten
1 tbsp soy sauce
4 spring onions,
    finely sliced

1 Mix the marinade ingredients in a small bowl. Place the pork in an ovenproof baking dish, pour over the marinade and cover the dish with cling film. Leave the pork to stand for at least 1 hour, turning the meat halfway through. Preheat the oven to 200°C/180°C Fan/Gas 6.

2 Roast the pork in the preheated oven for 40–45 minutes or until cooked through. Remove it from the oven, baste the meat with the reduced marinade in the dish, then cover it with foil and leave it to rest for 5 minutes.

3 While the pork is in the oven, cook the quinoa according to the packet instructions, then cool it as quickly as you can.

4 Heat a large non-stick frying pan, add the coconut oil, then the quinoa. Fry the quinoa for a minute or so, then add the peas and bean sprouts and continue to cook for 3–4 minutes. Push the quinoa to the side of the pan, then pour in the beaten eggs and stir so the egg breaks up. Add a dash of soy sauce, toss in the spring onions and fold everything together.

5 Slice the pork and serve with some quickly cooked pak choi or other greens and the fried quinoa.

Mince is generally sold in 500g packs so I suggest making a double quantity of burgers and keeping half for another day. Once you've shaped the burgers, put any extras between sheets of greaseproof paper and put them in the freezer. Make sure they are thoroughly thawed before using. Add a slice of Mexican-style cheese to your burgers if you like. MAKES 8

Lean and Mean Tex-Mex Burgers

2 tsp coconut oil
1 onion, very finely diced
3 garlic cloves, crushed
500g lean minced steak
500g lean turkey
    breast mince
1 tsp Dijon mustard
1 egg yolk
1 tsp ground cumin
1 tsp smoked paprika
sea salt
black pepper

To serve
2–4 wholemeal burger buns,
    halved and toasted
4 thin slices of Mexicana
    cheese (optional)
1 beef tomato, thickly sliced
1/2 red onion, sliced into
    rings (optional)
1 avocado, sliced
rocket leaves

1 Heat a teaspoon of oil in a frying pan and cook the onion and garlic for 5–6 minutes until softened, then set aside to cool.

2 Tip the onion and garlic into a bowl and add the steak and turkey mince, mustard, egg yolk, spices and seasoning. Mix well, then divide the mixture into 8 burgers, put them on a plate and leave them to chill in the fridge for 30 minutes. This helps to set the shape. At this point, freeze any burgers you're not going to use immediately. Preheat the oven to 190°C/170°C Fan/Gas 5.

3 Heat the remaining teaspoon of oil in an ovenproof frying pan and cook the burgers for about 5–6 minutes on each side. Put the pan in the preheated oven and cook for a further 10 minutes or until the burgers are cooked through. If you don't have an ovenproof pan, transfer the burgers to a baking tray and put them in the oven.

4 To serve, put each burger on a toasted bun half, top with a slice of cheese, if using, and garnish with slices of tomato, onion, avocado and a small handful of fresh rocket leaves. I prefer my burger without a bun on top, but that's up to you!

CHAPTER 6

SNACKS AND PACKED LUNCHES

Snacks are just as important as any other meal of the day; we often get hungry between meals, especially when active. Healthy snacking is something I've introduced into my routine over the last few years and the important thing is to watch the type of snacks we're eating. Out should go the crisps, chocolate, pastries and biscuits. In should come fruit, a small handful of nuts or even a boiled egg or two. Lots of kids are terrible about wanting to snack constantly, especially when it comes to sweeter treats, so make sure they are grazing on the right things. Feel free to tailor the flavours in these recipes to your family's liking and tweak them to taste.

As with everything in this book, preparation is the key. There really isn't any excuse not to have some healthy snacks to hand. A small tub of my spiced almonds or some of my mini frittatas are easy to make and keep the hunger pains at bay.

Many of these recipes also make great packed lunches. Try taking the beet hummus or minted pea salsa to work, together with a box of raw veg sticks or pitta chips. And I'm sure you'll also love my brie, avocado and sunblush tomato sandwiches – they beat the supermarket offerings every time.

Kale is great. I eat loads and use it in my juices, but this is my favourite way to enjoy it. Little ones love snacking on crisps but we all know how much salt and fat they contain. These kale chips are delicious, crunchy and a great alternative to regular crisps. You can adjust the seasoning to your taste and experiment with different flavours, but I guarantee that once you start making these you won't stop.

Sesame Kale Chips

100g kale
1 tsp olive oil
1 tsp soy sauce
grated zest of $1/2$ lemon
1 tbsp sesame seeds
sea salt
black pepper

1 Preheat the oven to 180°C/160°C Fan/Gas 4. Wash the kale, then tear bite-sized pieces from the tough stems. Dry them on kitchen paper – it's very important that the kale is completely dry.

2 Put the kale pieces in a bowl and drizzle them with the oil and soy sauce. Toss until all the kale is well coated, then add the lemon zest, sesame seeds, salt and pepper.

3 Line a baking tray with foil or baking parchment. Tip the kale on to the tray and bake in the preheated oven for 12–15 minutes until dried out and crispy. Best enjoyed right away.

Almonds are packed full of nutrients and make a perfect snack when you're on the go – and they taste amazing. These spiced-up almonds will keep you away from the bad stuff, like crisps and chocolate.

Smoky Spiced Almonds

200g whole almonds
1 tbsp coconut oil
1/2 tsp ground cumin
1/2 tsp smoked paprika
1/2 tsp chilli powder
  (optional)
1 tsp sea salt
1/2 tsp black pepper

1 Heat a large frying pan over a medium heat. Add the nuts and toast them for a couple of minutes until browned. Watch them carefully so they don't burn.

2 Keeping the pan on the heat, add the coconut oil and toss briefly until the nuts are coated with oil. Then add the spices and seasoning and toss again to coat. Tip the nuts out on to a plate, allow them to cool slightly, then enjoy.

These small eggy snacks are a treat at any time of day. You can also add any ingredients you have knocking around in the fridge or cupboard, such as a red pepper, some cherry tomatoes or a few slices of chorizo. They can be stored in the fridge in an airtight container for a couple of days, but they don't last that long when I'm around! MAKES 6

Mini Ham and Egg Frittatas

coconut oil, for greasing
6 slices of Parma or
　Serrano ham
4 free-range eggs
2 spring onions, thinly sliced
50g Cheddar cheese, grated
sea salt
black pepper

1 Preheat the oven to 200°C/180°C Fan/Gas 6. Lightly grease a 6-hole muffin or Yorkshire pudding tin with coconut oil.

2 Place a slice of ham in each hole and shape it to make a cup. Beat the eggs in a jug, season with salt and pepper and stir in the cheese and spring onions.

3 Carefully pour the egg mixture into the ham-lined cups and bake in the preheated oven for 12–14 minutes or until the eggs have set. Remove the frittatas from the tin and cool them on a rack.

An onion bhaji from my local takeaway is a guilty pleasure of mine, but the calories in them do start to add up. My one-pan version uses minimal oil, with a slightly longer than usual cooking time, and the results are great. Served with a lightly curried slaw in a wholemeal wrap, these crispy onion bhajis are the snack of kings! **SERVES 4**

Onion Bhaji Wrap with Coronation Slaw

2 red onions, thinly sliced
2 wholemeal burger buns, halved and toasted
2 garlic cloves, crushed
1 tbsp grated fresh root ginger
1 tbsp garam masala
1 tsp fennel seeds crushed
1/2 tsp turmeric
50g wholewheat flour
30ml water
2 tbsp coconut oil
4 wholemeal tortilla wraps
salad leaves, to serve
sea salt
black pepper

Coronation slaw
1/2 red cabbage, shredded
1 small red onion, very finely sliced
1 small carrot, grated
2 tbsp chopped fresh coriander
100ml low-fat natural yoghurt
1/2 tsp garam masala
50g raisins

1 Mix the onions with the garlic and ginger in a bowl and add the spices and flour. Add just enough water to bring the mixture together – about 30ml – and season with salt and pepper.

2 Heat the oil in a medium-sized frying pan, pour in the onion mixture and cook over a medium heat for 3–4 minutes. Flip the mixture over and continue cooking until it's golden, crispy and cooked through. I like to keep breaking the mixture up and reshaping it to get my bhaji crispy right through. The total cooking time will probably be about 20 minutes.

3 Place all the slaw ingredients in a bowl and mix well. Season with salt and pepper.

4 Portion the bhaji into 4, then divide between the wraps. Spoon on some slaw and finish with some salad leaves. Wrap and enjoy as a snack, or parcel up for a scrumptious packed lunch.

Falafels in pitta bread were my snack of choice after hitting the town on a night out when I was younger. Somehow I felt less guilty after eating these than if I demolished a greasy kebab. Now I find that these crispy balls of spiced chickpeas make a great snack. I like to eat mine with hummus and some tahini sauce (available in supermarkets) or you can add a splash of chilli sauce if you are feeling daring! **SERVES 4**

Crispy Falafels in Pitta

1 x 400g can of chickpeas, drained and rinsed
2 garlic cloves, crushed
1 tsp ground cumin
1 tsp ground coriander
1 tsp harissa paste
2 tbsp chopped fresh parsley
1 tbsp wholemeal flour
3 tbsp coconut oil
sea salt
black pepper

To serve
4 wholewheat pitta breads
1 tub of hummus
½ red onion, sliced
salad leaves
tahini sauce
lemon wedges

1 Put the chickpeas, garlic, spices, harissa, parsley and flour in a food processor and blitz until the mixture has a fine consistency. Tip it all into a bowl, season, then roll the mixture into about 12 small balls. Put these in the fridge for half an hour or so to set the shape.

2 Heat the oil in a frying pan, add the falafels and cook for 5–6 minutes or until golden all over.

3 Warm the pitta breads and split them open. Smear with some hummus, then stuff in some salad leaves. Add a few falafels, then garnish with some red onion. Drizzle over some tahini sauce and serve with lemon wedges.

I first tried this sensational flavour combination in a sandwich while on a long driving trip to Cornwall to check out universities with some college mates. The intense burst of flavour from the sunblush tomatoes was a revelation and I've used and enjoyed them in my recipes ever since. These sandwiches make a perfect packed lunch. SERVES 4

Brie, Avocado and Sunblush Tomato Sandwiches

150g sunblush tomatoes
olive oil (optional)
2 ripe avocados, stoned
   and peeled
8 slices of wholemeal bread
juice of 1/2 lime (optional)
200g Brie, thinly sliced
sea salt
black pepper

1 Place the tomatoes in a blender or food processor and pulse them until smooth. Add a little olive oil if you like to help break them down. This might seem a bit of a faff but processing the tomatoes makes them go a lot further.

2 Remove the stones from the avocados, scoop the flesh into a bowl and mash it well. Season with salt and pepper and, if preparing this in advance, add a squeeze of lime juice to stop the avocado flesh turning brown.

3 Divide the avocado between 4 slices of bread and add a portion of tomatoes. Lay on some slices of Brie, then top with the remaining slices of bread.

Use this recipe for toasted Mexican sandwiches made with tortillas as a base, but feel free to try adding your own favourite ingredients. I love to include a little fresh chilli in mine for a fiery kick, but that's up to you. The important part of this recipe is the cheese, which binds the other ingredients together as it melts. SERVES 4

Black Bean Quesadillas

100g chorizo, diced
1 red onion, finely sliced
1 x 400g can of black beans, drained and rinsed
1 x 198g can of sweetcorn, drained
1/2 green chilli, very finely diced (optional)
3 tbsp chopped fresh coriander
8 wholemeal tortillas
150g Cheddar cheese, grated
sea salt
black pepper

1 Fry the chorizo and onion in a dry pan for 5 minutes. Add the beans, sweetcorn and chilli, if using, and cook for another 2–3 minutes. Stir in the fresh coriander and season with salt and pepper.

2 Place a quarter of the mixture on top of 1 of the tortillas and spread it into a thin layer, then sprinkle over some cheese. Top with another tortilla and toast the sandwich in a dry non-stick pan over a medium heat for 1–2 minutes on each side. Repeat with the remaining ingredients. Serve your quesadillas with some fresh guacamole if you like.

I'm a massive fan of raw food. Cooking destroys some nutrients so it's really good to eat lots of raw veg. This colourful snack is great to enjoy at home or for a packed lunch and it's very quick and easy to make. The kids will love it too. Don't think I'm going all posh on you with the French name – crudités just means uncooked food but sounds a bit more exciting than chopped raw veg. You will find similar dips in your supermarket, but have a look at the labels to see how much salt and sugars they contain and you may well be shocked! **SERVES 4**

Beet Hummus with Crudités

400g can of chickpeas, drained and rinsed
1 beetroot, peeled and roughly chopped
2 garlic cloves, crushed
40ml extra virgin olive oil, plus extra for drizzling
3 tbsp tahini
juice of $\frac{1}{2}$ lemon
$\frac{1}{2}$ tsp cumin
sea salt
black pepper

Crudités
1 carrot, peeled
1 yellow or red pepper, deseeded
$\frac{1}{2}$ cucumber
cherry tomatoes
bunch of radishes

1 Put the ingredients for the beet hummus, except for the salt and pepper, in a food processor and blitz to a fine paste. Season with salt and pepper, then taste and add more cumin and lemon juice if you think it needs it. Spoon into a serving bowl and drizzle with some more extra virgin olive oil.

2 Cut the carrot, pepper and cucumber into batons, add some cherry tomatoes and radishes and dip away.

We all love to snack so the trick is to make the right choices. Instead of reaching for a bag of tortilla chips, try my baked pitta version. These are perfect with the minted pea salsa and also great with a fresh and zingy tomato salsa. **SERVES 4**

Minted Pea Salsa and Baked Pitta Chips

200g frozen peas, defrosted
50g feta cheese, finely diced
1/2 red onion, finely diced
1/2 red chilli, deseeded and finely diced (optional)
2 tbsp finely chopped fresh mint
30ml extra virgin olive oil
juice of 1/2 lime
4 wholemeal pitta breads
sea salt
black pepper

1 To make the pea salsa, crush the peas in a bowl and add the feta, onion, chilli, if using, and mint. Mix well, then stir in the oil and lime juice and season with salt and pepper.

2 Preheat the oven to 190°C/170° Fan/Gas 5. Cut each pitta bread into rough triangle shapes and spread them on a baking tray. Cook in the preheated oven for 10 minutes or until golden, then cool slightly and use them to scoop up the salsa.

Popcorn makes a great snack to keep hunger at bay. I'm a huge fan of these Japanese flavours and I'm guessing if you've ever eaten sushi, then you will have tried the combination of fiery wasabi and ginger. Just don't do what my friend did once and mistake a dollop of wasabi for a mushy pea. Hot stuff! Obviously the horseradish-like flavour of the wasabi may be a little too much for young palates so feel free to leave it out.

Wasabi and Ginger Popcorn

2 tbsp coconut oil
100g unpopped kernels
1 heaped tsp wasabi paste
1 tbsp soy sauce
1/2 tsp ground ginger
1 tsp black sesame seeds

1 Place the largest pan you have over a medium to high heat. Add a teaspoon of coconut oil, then the kernels and stir to coat all of the kernels evenly. Cover the pan with a tight-fitting lid. Once you hear the corn popping, reduce the heat to low and shake the pan occasionally until the popping stops. Pour the popcorn into a bowl.

2 Heat the remaining oil, then add in the wasabi, soy and ginger and mix until combined. Add this to the popcorn and stir to coat the kernels evenly before sprinkling over the sesame seeds.

CHAPTER 7

DESSERTS

I've got a serious sweet tooth. It's my Achilles heel when it comes to eating well and I know I shouldn't be feeding myself and my family sugary and fatty desserts too often. Sometimes I can keep my cravings at bay by eating a couple of squares of dark chocolate or a handful of frozen grapes, but there are times where only a rich pudding will do, like my comforting fruit crumble or an indulgent raspberry cheesecake pot. I've also thrown in an adults-only treat – my Mojito granita, which is refreshing and delicious.

To keep the recipes as healthy as possible, I've cut back on the fat and refined sugar content and relied on naturally sweet ingredients. Obviously these desserts aren't completely sin free but hey – everything in moderation, right?

These little parcels are like mini strudels – crisp golden pastry on the outside and bursting with fruity goodness on the inside. I use a small amount of butter in this recipe to help crisp up the pastry, but coconut oil will do the same job if you prefer it. I like to serve these samosas with a dollop of sharp Greek yoghurt, which cuts through the sweetness of the fruity filling. SERVES 4

Apple and Raisin Samosas

1 tsp coconut oil
200g Bramley apples, peeled and diced
200g Braeburn apples, peeled and diced
1/2 tsp ground cinnamon
1–2 tbsp maple syrup
50g raisins
grated zest of 1/2 lemon
4 sheets of filo pastry, cut in half lengthways
20g unsalted butter or coconut oil, melted
icing sugar, for dusting

1 Put the coconut oil in a saucepan, add the apples, cinnamon and syrup and place the pan over a low to medium heat. Cook gently for 10 minutes until the apples have softened. Take the pan off the heat, add the raisins and lemon zest and leave to cool.

2 Preheat the oven to 180°C/160°C Fan/Gas 4. Take a sheet of filo, brush it with melted butter or coconut oil and fold it over to make a long rectangle. Brush with more butter, then place a large spoonful of the apple mixture on the bottom left-hand side of the pastry. Fold from corner to corner until the mixture is fully enclosed. Repeat until you've used all the filo and apple mix.

3 Place the samosas on a greased baking tray and bake them for 20–25 minutes or until golden brown. Leave the samosas to cool for 10 minutes, then dust with icing sugar and serve.

We love a good luxurious slice of cake in our house. Baking can be a little tricky at times, as it's a very precise science. I'm much more of a throw-it-all-in-and-see-what-happens type of cook at home so this quick and easy cake goes down a treat. It's so simple, in fact, that my daughter Indie likes to get involved when I make it. The carrot and courgette give the cake a fabulous moist texture while packing in extra vitamins and nutrients. Perfect with a cup of tea or in a lunchbox. SERVES 8

Hide the Veg Carrot and Courgette Cake

Dry ingredients
180g dark muscovado sugar
200g self-raising flour
1 tsp bicarbonate of soda
1 heaped tsp mixed spice
1 tsp ground cinnamon
small grating of nutmeg
100g walnuts, crushed
    slightly but left chunky
pinch of salt

Wet ingredients
150ml olive oil, plus
    extra for greasing
2 eggs
100g carrots, grated
100g courgette, grated
finely grated zest of
    1 orange

Frosting
120g unsalted butter,
    softened
280g light cream cheese
60g icing sugar
walnuts, to decorate

1 Preheat the oven to 190°C/170°C Fan/Gas 5. Grease a 900g loaf tin with oil and line it with baking parchment.

2 Mix the dry ingredients in a bowl until thoroughly combined. In a separate bowl, whisk together the olive oil and eggs, then stir this mixture into the dry ingredients. Add the grated carrots, courgette and zest and mix until combined.

3 Pour the mixture into the prepared tin, then place the tin on a baking tray and bake for 50–60 minutes or until a skewer comes out clean. Remove the cake from the oven and leave to cool slightly, then turn it out on to a wire rack to cool completely.

4 In a large bowl or a food mixer, beat the softened butter and cream cheese together until smooth, then stir in the icing sugar. Place the frosting in a piping bag and pipe it on top of the cooled cake. Decorate with walnuts before serving.

I love the flavours of the Caribbean, which is one of my favourite places in the world. This is a classic combo – for me, taste treats don't get much better than this juicy pineapple bursting in my mouth. For a super-quick version without the rum, simply add the raisins to some Greek yoghurt and stir in the honey. **SERVES 4**

Vanilla-baked Pineapple with Rum and Raisin Greek Yoghurt

50g raisins
20ml rum (optional)
150ml 0% fat Greek yoghurt
1 tbsp honey
1 pineapple
1 vanilla pod
1 tsp coconut oil or butter
coconut shavings, to serve

1 Put the raisins in a small bowl, add the rum and leave them to soak for about 30 minutes. Put the yoghurt in a separate bowl, add the honey, then stir in the soaked raisins and rum. Put the yoghurt in the fridge until needed.

2 Peel the pineapple, then remove the little 'eyes'. Cut the pineapple into segments lengthways, discarding the tough central core. Split the vanilla pod in half lengthways and scrape out the sticky black seeds with a small spoon, then rub the seeds over the pineapple segments.

3 Preheat the oven to 180°C/160°C Fan/Gas 4. Heat the oil or butter in an ovenproof frying pan. Add the pineapple segments and fry them gently until lightly coloured, then put the pan in the oven for 15–20 minutes. If you don't have an ovenproof pan, just transfer the pineapple segments to a baking tray.

4 Serve the pineapple with a dollop of the Greek yoghurt and some shavings of coconut.

These fluffy pancakes are American-style – light, thick and full of flavour. Any kind of fruit goes well with them, such as blueberries, raspberries or even stewed rhubarb, but when cherries are in season there is no better choice for me. A quick drizzle of dark chocolate is all you need, but for pure indulgence a scoop of frozen yoghurt is the business. This recipe makes about 12 small pancakes. **SERVES 4**

Buttermilk Pancakes with Cherries and Chocolate Drizzle

250g wholewheat
  self-raising flour
1 tsp bicarbonate of soda
80g golden caster sugar
3 small eggs, beaten
300ml buttermilk
50g butter, melted, plus
  a small knob of butter
70g dark chocolate
  (70% cocoa)
200g cherries, halved
  and pitted

1 In a large bowl, sift the flour, bicarbonate of soda and sugar. In a separate bowl, whisk the eggs with the buttermilk, then add this mixture to the dry ingredients. Whisk, then add the melted butter.

2 Set the oven at its lowest temperature to keep the pancakes warm as you cook them. Warm a large non-stick frying pan over a medium heat. Add a small knob of butter and place 4 small ladlefuls of batter into the pan, then leave them to cook for about 2 minutes. Flip the pancakes and cook them for another couple of minutes. Pop them in the oven to keep warm, then repeat until you have used up all the batter.

3 Bring a saucepan of water to a gentle simmer. Break the chocolate into small pieces and place them in a bowl that fits over the pan but does not touch the water. Leave until the chocolate has melted, then carefully remove the bowl from the pan.

4 Stack the pancakes on a serving plate, scatter over the cherries and drizzle with melted chocolate.

If you have kids and they are anything like Indie, my little one, then you know how much they can nag for something sweet. Don't get me wrong, though, I'm not against my daughter having a sweet treat every now and then, especially when I know exactly what's in it. Frozen fruit is a great standby and I freeze grapes for her (and me) to pick at when a craving comes along. She loves these pops too. They require freezing overnight and you'll need some lolly sticks. **SERVES 4**

Chocolate-dipped Banana Pops

2 bananas
100g dark chocolate
    (70% cocoa)
50g chopped nuts (I like
    pistachios and almonds)

1 Peel the bananas and cut them in half at the centre point. Insert a lolly stick up through each piece of banana from the cut end, place the bananas on a tray and pop them in the freezer overnight.

2 Bring a saucepan of water to a gentle simmer. Break the chocolate into small pieces and place them in a bowl that fits over the pan but does not touch the water. Leave until the chocolate has melted, then carefully remove the bowl from the pan.

3 Transfer the chocolate to a tall glass, then dip the bananas in 1 at a time. Sprinkle with the nuts and enjoy.

This recipe was inspired by a like-minded friend, Helen Fospero. She regularly puts herself down regarding her cooking skills, or lack of them, but she is inspirational in her passion for giving her kids good food. If we're honest, we all love a pud now and then, and if it can be as guilt free as this then we're on to a winner! Cheers Helen. **SERVES 4**

Cheat's Frozen Banana and Peanut Butter Ice Cream

6 ripe bananas
1–2 heaped tbsp
   unsweetened
   peanut butter
80ml milk or almond milk
2 tbsp raisins
chocolate sauce, for
   drizzling (optional)

1 Peel and chop the bananas, put them on a tray and place them in the freezer for 1–2 hours or until frozen.

2 Once the bananas are frozen, take them out and blitz them in a blender with the peanut butter and enough milk to get the consistency you like. Spoon the mixture into bowls, then top with the raisins and a small drizzle of chocolate sauce if you are feeling extra indulgent.

A fruit-packed crumble is a British classic. My nutty version is healthier than usual, as it's not loaded up with flour, butter and sugar. Any fruit that's bang in season works perfectly, including rhubarb, gooseberries, pears – you get the idea. Obviously the tarter the fruit the more sugar you'll need to balance the flavours. I've used a combination of apples – the Bramleys for texture and Braeburns for sweetness. **SERVES 4**

Apple and Blackberry Nut Crumble

1 tsp coconut oil
200g Bramley apples, peeled, cored and cut into 2.5cm pieces
200g Braeburn apples, peeled, cored and cut into 2.5cm pieces
1 small piece of stem ginger, chopped
100g blackberries
1/2 tsp ground cinnamon
1–2 tbsp honey or maple syrup, to taste

Crumble topping
100g rolled oats
100g almonds, crushed
2 tbsp coconut oil, melted
2 tbsp honey or maple syrup

1 First make the topping. Preheat the oven to 200°C/180°C Fan/Gas 6. Put the oats, almonds, oil and honey or maple syrup in a bowl and mix until well combined. Scatter the mixture over a baking tray and bake for 15–20 minutes or until golden.

2 Warm the teaspoon of coconut oil in a pan and add the apples, ginger, blackberries and cinnamon. Cook gently for about 10 minutes, then add the honey or maple syrup to taste.

3 Divide the fruit mixture into ramekins, top with crumble topping and enjoy.

These tiffin bites are rich, chewy and indulgent – I find that one is never enough. I must confess that chocolate is my weakness, but sometimes a small taste of the good dark stuff is enough to ward off my sweet cravings. If I'm making this for kids, I use half dark, half milk chocolate, as the all-dark version is quite bitter – just how I like it. MAKES 20 SQUARES

Fruit and Nut Tiffin Bites

50g unsalted butter, plus extra for greasing
250g dark chocolate (70% cocoa), broken into pieces
50g coconut oil
60g honey
60g organic popped rice
100g dried mixed berries, such as cherries, blueberries, cranberries
100g macadamia nuts, roughly chopped

1 Grease a 20cm square tin with butter and line it with cling film, leaving some cling film hanging over the sides of the tin to make it easier to remove the tiffin.

2 Bring a saucepan of water to a gentle simmer. Put the chocolate, butter, coconut oil and honey in a bowl that fits over the pan but does not touch the water. Leave until everything has melted, then stir well to combine and carefully remove the bowl from the pan.

3 Put the popped rice, dried fruit and nuts in a large bowl, pour in the melted chocolate mixture and stir until well mixed. Spoon the mixture into the baking tin and press it down into an even layer with the bottom of a glass. Place it in the fridge and leave to set for at least 4 hours.

4 Lift the tiffin out of the tin with the help of the cling film and place it on a board. Allow it to come up to room temperature, then slice it into 20 squares.

These cheesecake pots combine a crunchy nutty base with a light creamy filling studded with fresh raspberries – strawberries or blueberries work well too. They taste rich and luxurious but they're not heavy, and I keep the portions small so I can satisfy my sweet tooth without too much of a guilt trip. They're quick and easy to make and I often knock them up for the family while waiting for the Sunday roast to cook. **SERVES 4**

Raspberry Cheesecake Pots

60g nuts, such as almonds
  or hazelnuts
20g coconut oil, melted
1 tbsp honey
150g light cream cheese
100ml Greek yoghurt
2 tbsp honey
100g fresh raspberries

Raspberry sauce
100g raspberries
1 tbsp honey, to taste
20ml water
small squeeze of lemon juice

1 Put the nuts in a food processor and blitz to break them down to fine crumbs. Tip the crumbs into a bowl and mix in the melted coconut oil and honey until fully incorporated. Place this mixture into ramekins or small jars, press it down well, then place the ramekins in the fridge to set for 20 minutes.

2 Put the cream cheese, yoghurt and honey in a bowl and mix with a hand whisk until smooth.

3 Take the ramekins out of the fridge and divide the raspberries over the biscuit base. Spoon the cheese mixture over the top until the raspberries are completely covered. Chill in the fridge for 2 hours.

4 To make the raspberry sauce, put the raspberries, honey and water in a small pan. Warm over a gentle heat for about 10 minutes until the berries have broken down, then add the lemon juice to balance the flavours. Leave to cool.

5 When you're ready to eat, pour some raspberry sauce over each little pot and serve at once.

When figs are in season, they're a joy to eat. They're at their very best in the autumn months and quickly roasting them brings out their natural sweetness. I like to use pistachios in this recipe but chopped almonds or hazelnuts would also be great. If you really want to push the boat out, add a small splash of amaretto – it's lush! **SERVES 4**

Baked Figs with Honey and Pistachios

15g unsalted butter
12 ripe figs
1–2 tbsp runny honey
   or maple syrup
unsalted pistachios, shelled
Greek yoghurt, to serve

1 Preheat the oven to 180°C/160°C Fan/Gas 4. Grease a shallow ovenproof dish with the butter.

2 Trim the stalks off the figs, then make 2 vertical cuts from the tops down the sides. Don't cut all the way through. Give the bottom of each fig a quick squeeze to open it out and place the figs in the buttered dish.

3 Drizzle the honey over the figs and sprinkle with pistachios. Bake for 15–20 minutes, then serve with a dollop of Greek yoghurt.

I first came across mojitos while on a trip to Cuba and I've never tasted better, but this granita comes damn close in the refreshment stakes. It may be a bit of a faff to make but it's so worth it. There's nothing difficult, although you do need to check the granita every half hour to break up the ice crystals. Obviously this is for adults only but you could leave out the rum for a kid-friendly version. I made this as a treat for the adults after Indie's last birthday party and it went down very well! SERVES 8-10

Mojito Granita

600ml just-boiled water
100g golden caster sugar
juice of 6 limes
grated zest of 1 lime
60ml white rum
5 drops of Angostura
    bitters (optional)
small handful of fresh mint,
    very finely chopped
lime wedges, to serve

1 Pour the water into a bowl, add the sugar and stir to dissolve. Leave to cool, then add the lime juice, zest, rum, Angostura bitters and mint. Pour the mixture into a chilled baking dish and place it in the freezer.

2 After 30 minutes, take the dish out and use a fork to pull any crystals away from the sides of the container. Put it back in the freezer and keep checking it every 30 minutes, forking through and breaking up any crystals. Repeat until you have a container of fluffy crystals. This will take 4–5 hours.

3 If not serving the granita straight away, scrape it into a plastic container with a lid and store it in the freezer. Remove 20 minutes before serving and garnish with a wedge of lime on the side. Another serving idea is to hollow out the flesh from some lime halves and serve the granita in those.

Index

THANK YOU!

To have written and published one cookbook was the stuff of dreams, but to be asked to do a second is something else. But of course it's not all down to me. Without the help of many, many people this book simply would not have been possible so here goes, and please forgive me if I've missed anyone out.

My family – I might take you all for granted at times, but I know that you are always there for me when I need advice, inspiration or just an ear to bend or bore. Lou, you are still a massive inspiration and part of my life, and also gave me the biggest reason to do any of this – my fast-growing daughter Indie-Roux, who drives me to do something with my life. I know she's not too bothered at the moment, but I hope that one day she will be able to look back and be proud of me.

To Jan Croxson, Borra Garson and the team at Deborah McKenna Ltd for looking after me and out for me for nearly 10 years. You have been stars!

Another person who deserves a great big thank you is the lovely Sue Walton, who gambled on me six years ago by giving me a shot at ITV. I've enjoyed every single minute since, and it's amazing to finally work for you again. I hope you know how much you have done to change my life.

I would also like to thank a few special people from the ITV *Lorraine* show: Emma Gormley and of course the amazing Lorraine Kelly for being brave enough to taste my recipes. I know eating curry at 8:30am might be a struggle for anyone! Then there are my food producers, Sarah and Kate. You are saints to put up with us lot. Thanks for keeping me organized and for all of the support.

Thanks to everyone at Transworld for their support but especially to Rebecca and Doug. You have been great! I was blessed to have the same team with me when shooting my second book so thank you to amazing photographer Martin Poole, Smith & Gilmour for their classy design, Aya Nishimura, Xenia Von Oswald and Sam Dixon for making the food look so mouthwatering, and Tamzin Ferdinando for the beautiful props. And to Jinny Johnson – thanks again for making this experience as easy as it has been, especially for someone without a GCSE in English! You have all been fantastic and far exceeded my expectations, again and again.